RAGTOPS

Classic American convertibles of the fifties and sixties

RAGTOPS

Classic American convertibles of the fifties and sixties

THIERRY EMPTAS   **FRANCOIS LEMEUNIER**

Motorbooks International
Publishers & Wholesalers ®

This edition published in 1989 by Motorbooks International
Publishers & Wholesalers, P O Box 2, 729 Prospect Avenue,
Osceola, WI 54020 USA

First published by Editions Presse Audiovisuel, Paris, 1989
© Editions Presse Audiovisuel, 1989

Printed and bound in France

Library of Congress Cataloging-in-Publication Data
    Emptas, Thierry.
    Ragtops.
    Translation of: Cabriolets américaines.
    1. Automobiles, Convertible—United States—History.
I. Le Meunier, Francois.   II. Title.
TL23.B2313   1989   629.222   89-8261
ISBN 0-87938-373-9

Acknowledgments

Foreword

It was only possible to present the cars that appear in this book thanks to the great kindness of European and American collectors and to the help given to us by many clubs.

We extend our warm thanks to the Packard-Club International, the Amicale Packard France (Mr. de Lorgeril), Mr. Schreiber, Mr. Gaudfroy, Mr. Imbert, Mr. Hassan, the Cadillac-Club de Suisse (Mr. Zimmerman and Mr. Vonaesh), Mr. de Montremy, Auto-Folies (Mr. Rigoli and Mr. Coudert), Mr. Dufour, the Mustang-Club de France (Mr. Serpagli and Mr. Le Tellier), Restaur-Auto (Mr. Cointreau), Mr. Robba, the American Car-Club de France (Mr. Petitpres), the Corvair-Club de France (Mrs. Poudroux and Mr. Dupuis), the Amicale Studebaker de France, Mr. Bader and the Voiturium (Mr. Heidet).

In particular, we would also like to thank Mr. and Mrs. Yount of the Edsel-Club International, who enabled us to meet many American collectors, and Mr. Van Der Stricht, who was of particular help to us in our work.

The nicknames and slurs slung at the great American convertibles of the fifties and sixties have become almost as famous as the cars themselves. Some laughingly called them Land Yachts. Or Dream Boats. Pregnant Whales. Pontoons. Bathtubs. Yet most people remember them affectionately as simple Ragtops.

The fifties and sixties were curious times in America. The fifties was a decade stereotyped as complacent and conforming; the sixties were turbulent and frenzied, a time of change. Gripped by these forces, the American auto makers dreamt up cars in the image of the eras—voluptuous and opulent in the fifties, powerful and sleek in the sixties. But whether the times were good or bad, the cars they engendered were tremendous.

And then, at 10:12 a.m. on April 21, 1976, the last American convertible was built. Fittingly, it was a Cadillac Eldorado, the make and model that had symbolized luxurious cabriolet to so many. Surprisingly, however, it was painted not in funeral black, but in pearly white. This last run of convertibles was bought up by eager collectors across the country, bemoaning the demise of the great ragtop.

As everyone now knows—and as many sensed at the time—it was not truly the end. And indeed, the popularity of current American convertibles, such as the modern Corvette, testify to America's undying love for the ragtop.

To enable you to share in the excitement, we invite you on a journey through the history of the great American convertibles. Sitting comfortably on wide moleskin seats, we will drive past the famed founders: Harley J. Earl, Raymond Loewy and Virgil Exner, Charles F. Kettering and, closer to home, Lee Iacocca. These were the extravagant fifties, when the weight of the chrome and the height of the tail fins were a measure of social success. And the wild sixties, with the dawn of the convertible for everyone, the Mustang.

So now push the pearly button to open the electric top, put the automatic gearshift into Drive and let yourself be carried along by the silent power of the big V-8.

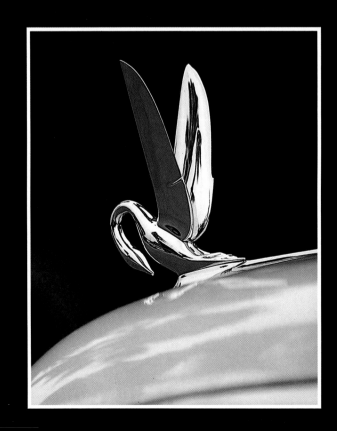

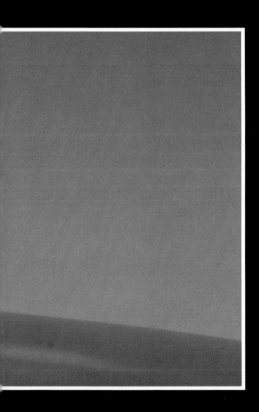

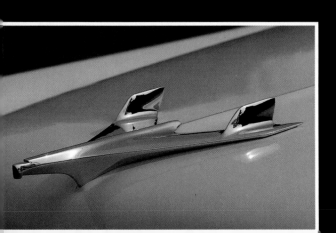

Contents

1948 Chrysler Town & Country

Dry-land yacht

If automobiles fascinate you because of their performance and mechanical beauty, skip these few pages—the Chrysler Town & Country is not for you. The Town & Country is first and foremost a sumptuous convertible, with a body like that of a yacht, lines reminiscent of the thirties and a long hood dominating a blissfully grinning radiator.

In 1948, the luxury and refinement offered by this car enabled it to rival the biggest names of the automobile world. Its seats were covered with a pleasant blend of leather and cloth. Behind the immense steering wheel was a monumental dashboard, the throne for an immense radio that changed color depending on the channel selected—as did the speedometer: green up to 30 mph, orange up to 50 mph and red thereafter! Finally, Chrysler installed a small mirror at the bottom of the windshield just in front of the driver; when the top closed the driver could still see the traffic lights at junctions without getting a stiff neck!

The car still had an old in-line eight-cylinder engine, a mass of cast iron as heavy as an anvil, with 323 ci and no

1948 Chrysler Town & Country

more than 135 horsepower. No matter—the Town & Country did not intend to race itself at Indianapolis and in any case, the sumptuous balance between the luxury and the phenomenal torque of 270 lb-ft, generously delivered at 1600 rpm, allowed it to glide smoothly and quietly along.

To retrace the origin of this woodie, we must go back to the early forties. After the failure of the amazing Airflow, which troubled the conscience of America, Chrysler retreated into its shell and brought out cars that were somewhat lacking in imagination. Although this conservatism did not prevent the company's popular models from defending their positions, the top-of-the-line Crown Imperials encountered increasing difficulties, particularly when faced with the Packards and Cadillacs, already equipped with V-8 engines. It was then that Chrysler decided to attack the woodie market, which Ford and Chevrolet shared.

At the time, woodies were no more than station wagons with wooden bodies. Why station wagons? Simply because woodies had always been utilitarian vehicles, destined for the rural environment, with wood being used in their manufacture only for reasons of simplicity. But in the early forties, their rustic appearance had become increasingly attractive to urbanites, who succumbed to the cars' country charms. Therefore, in 1941 and 1942, the Chrysler catalog included two Town & Country station wagons.

The situation changed after World War II, when Chrysler decided to market a complete series of Town & Country models: sedans, hardtop coupes and convertibles. Thanks to Chrysler, the woodie was becoming a luxury item for an affluent clientele. Six different models were originally planned, but only three were eventually produced: a six- or eight-cylinder sedan and a convertible delivered exclusively with the larger engine. From 1947 on, Chrysler retained only the six-cylinder sedan and the convertible. The convertible gave the Town & Country a permanent place in legend and opened up the grand driveways of Hollywood to the woodies. Esther Williams, the nymph in *Million Dollar Mermaid,* succumbed to the warm and soft reflections of the car's paneling.

From the back, the curves of this Chrysler Town & Country give it a thirties feel. From the front, the radiator grille spreads a dazzling, chrome-plated smile across the entire width of the car.

1948 Chrysler Town & Country

Whereas the uprights were made of ash, chosen for its dimensional stability, the panels were made of mahogany from Honduras. Unfortunately, exoticism costs money, and this noble species was replaced in 1947 by an imitation made from adhesive paper!

Despite its intricate woodwork, which required great attention to detail and a build rate incompatible with mass production, the Town & Country convertible was no more expensive than its competitors. In 1948, it cost only $3,395, coming to within a few dollars of the 62 Series Cadillac or the Packard Super Eight. Yet production still remained limited: 1,935 convertibles in 1946, 3,136 in 1947 and 3,309 in 1948. As for the sedan, after an enviable score of 4,124 units in 1946, production fell to 2,651 in 1947 and to only 1,175 in 1948.

In 1949, Chrysler unveiled its new line. Although the pontoon look was gaining ground, the Town & Country disappeared into oblivion. The new range retained only the convertible, but the panels with their reddish reflections had disappeared. Only the ash uprights remained.

Chrysler produced another 1,000 Town & Countrys in 1949, and its total fell to 700 in 1950, the last year of production, when the convertible was abandoned in favor of an elegant hardtop coupe. But Chrysler hardly cared about the fate of the Town & Countrys. The head office was much too busy tightening the last bolts on a bombshell that was to burst on the scene the following year. And in 1951, the famous V-8 with overhead valves and hemi cylinder heads appeared, a wonderful piece of engineering that soon started a commercial war.

With the bright reflections of its ash uprights and the reddish sparkle of its mahogany panels, the Town & Country is a veritable yacht for the road. At the center of the dashboard, behind a chrome-plated and finely worked front, is the radio. It changes color according to the tone.

1948 Chevrolet Fleetmaster

Everyday service

Thomas H. Keating, Chevrolet's head of sales immediately following World War II, was enjoying a happy
period: customers were rushing to buy anything remotely
resembling an automobile. Another happy task in 1948 was
his honorary role as the starter in the Indianapolis 500.
Keating did not arrive empty-handed to the race, since the
pace car was a Fleetmaster convertible, which was offered to
the winner, Mauri Rose.

Chevrolet did not really need such promotion. The problem was not how to attract customers but how to produce
cars, and the firm therefore brought out its prewar lines,
virtually unchanged. These models had nothing revolutionary about them, but Chevrolet has always guarded
against bold innovation and aesthetic adventure. Its strength
is in cars that are simple, robust and inexpensive, while
remaining pleasing, attractively designed and well-equipped,
giving the customer the feeling of having received his or her
money's worth. The Styleline, Fleetmaster and Fleetline
took their place in this tradition. Whereas certain manufac-

1948 Chevrolet Fleetmaster

turers played at being sorcerer's apprentices with the pontoon style, the Chevys retained a more conventional appearance, more to the taste of their conservative working-class customers.

Under the hood was one of the most legendary figures of Detroit: the Cast Iron Wonder, the in-line six-cylinder engine launched by Chevrolet in 1929. In nineteen years of existence, this engine had gone from 194 to 216.5 ci and doubled its strength from 46 to 90 horsepower. This easygoing servant also made itself an impressive reputation for robustness. In 1940, young Juan Manuel Fangio won a marathon nearly 10,000 km in length, from Buenos Aires to Lima, Peru, at the wheel of a standard Chevy. Not until 1952 was this engine retired from service.

Of the eleven models included in its catalog in 1948, Chevrolet offered a convertible. Its classic style of relatively sober and harmonious decoration and almost European proportions combined to produce a neat and elegant car, attracting more than 20,000 customers. Apart from its aesthetic qualities, the Fleetmaster convertible was equipped with practical and pleasing features, such as a single key for the doors and the ignition. The dashboard was agreeably presented in sheet metal painted to imitate wood. It contained a complete set of instruments, including a speedometer, gas gauge, water temperature gauge, ammeter and oil pressure gauge. Furthermore, a large clock was placed in front of the passenger. Customers could enjoy the pleasures of this car for $1,750, only $10 more than the cost of an equivalent Ford convertible.

The struggle between Ford and Chevrolet had raged since the mid-twenties. But for the moment, Chevrolet had taken the leading place in the market and looked to the future with serenity, since new models were expected in 1949. Once again, the company was to play its favorite trump: cars that were full of good sense, attractive and robust at the same time. The Chevrolet had a constitution of iron, and this was all for the best, because if Chevrolet caught a cold, all of General Motors would sneeze.

The sensible and harmonious design of this Chevrolet Fleetmaster has inspired numerous European manufacturers. Look at the symmetry of the dashboard, painted imitation wood.

1948 Packard Custom Eight

Intoxicating charms
of aristocracy

The purists snicker at the 1948 Packard Custom Eight as a pregnant whale or an upturned bathtub. It's true that this model is not the most elegant one produced by the firm on East Grand Boulevard, but what does it matter? Whatever period it comes from, a Packard remains a Packard—and the name is still one of the finest symbols of the automobile aristocracy; it remains forever synonymous with refined luxury and exemplary quality.

Before World War II, Packard was one of the biggest. Unlike other prestigious makes, such as Cord, Auburn, Duesenberg, Marmon and Stutz, it managed to escape the whirlpool of the Great Depression of 1929. It was a bumpy passage, but chairman Alvan Macauley avoided the abyss by adapting to the market and offering more popular series of cars, thereby opening up the Packard dream to a new clientele.

Designed and assembled with the same attention to quality and presented with the same care, these new models—called the 120s (to which the 110s would later be added)—

1948 Packard Custom Eight

continued the tradition and image of the company, while allowing the manufacturer to record substantial profits. Thus, from their first appearance in January 1935 until they ceased production in February 1942, 479,630 "little" Packards left the factory, compared with 42,700 top-of-the-line models. The age of superstars seemed to have gone, and all future production would derive from the 110 and 120 models.

March 1941 saw the appearance of the Clipper, which, based on the 120, represented an important aesthetic step in the history of the make. Taking inspiration from a study by Darrin, Werner Gubitz, who had been officiating at Packard since the mid-twenties, and Charles Yeager sketched a modern and flexible line, whose style would nevertheless not put off the company's traditional clientele. One distinctive feature of this new design was the abandoning of the running board, which allowed the car to be made considerably wider. In 1942, the new-look style of Packard spread to most models in the range.

After World War II, the Clippers reappeared. Packard had devoted the years of conflict exclusively to producing engines, however, and the company had considerable difficulty restarting the assembly lines; despite the rush of orders, production was at a virtual standstill. In addition, the rules of the game had changed. Packard could no longer live on its reputation alone. The automobile was entering a period of merciless competition in a market where demand greatly exceeded supply. Therefore in 1947, in order to attract a clientele that was keen to forget four years of privation, Packard presented a completely redesigned range. Ed Macauley, vice-president of design, contented himself with lowering the lines of the Clippers and giving them the pontoon treatment. The result produced howls from the faithful purists. There was a stream of nicknames, and detractors reproached the good Macauley with having inflated the Clippers.

In the end, customers were much less severe. In 1948, Packard achieved a high score, selling 92,251 cars, easily outclassing Cadillac and Lincoln. Two convertibles were included in the catalog that year. The first was the Super Eight, built on a short chassis. The second belonged to the Custom series, the ultimate in Packard style.

Despite its nickname of "pregnant whale" this Packard has all the attractions of an aristocrat. The lattice-work radiator grille, reserved for the top-of-the-line models, hides a wonderfully balanced in-line eight-cylinder engine.

1948 Packard Custom Eight

In addition to its long wheelbase (127 inches, instead of 120), the 1949 Custom convertible was distinguished by its crisscrossed radiator grille—a characteristic feature of Custom models, whereas other series had to content themselves with horizontal bars. The car sported two lines of chrome trim at the bottom of the body and—the exclusive symbol of the top-of-the-line models—a superb cormorant ornament with spread wings at the end of the car's long hood. Despite its thickened appearance, this convertible still exuded the Packard know-how and good taste, and remained "a gentleman's car designed by gentlemen." The style of the dashboard was of exemplary sobriety, and the car was equipped with four hydraulically operated windows—a rare refinement at the time.

Despite its high price of $4,295, which made it one of the most expensive convertibles of the year alongside the Lincoln Continental at $4,746, 1,105 customers succumbed to the charms of this authentic aristocrat, not caring about its obsolete engine. Packard still believed in the virtues of its in-line eight-cylinder engine with side valves, 356 ci and 160 horsepower which had remained unchanged since 1940 and whose design dated back to the thirties! Although the engine's smoothness and balance still worked wonders, the company was being left dangerously far behind. The following year it suffered a severe blow with the appearance of Oldsmobile's and Cadillac's high-performance V-8s. The race for power had begun, and Packard did not manage to equip itself with the arms to counterattack in time.

In March 1948, Alvan Macauley, who had been president since 1916, retired. Whether it was a coincidence or a somber omen, this departure corresponded with the first signs of the company's death. Packard was to live through some more painful years, punctuated by spurts of creativity that were as superb as they were desperate.

With a total of 1,105 made, the Custom Eight convertible was the most expensive model in the Packard range in 1948. The car's slightly rigid dignity is reflected in the austere design of the dashboard.

1949 De Soto Custom

Simple pleasures

For many of the soldiers and sailors returning from World War II to start up a family in the spring of peacetime, the new De Soto was the car of their dreams. Prewar De Sotos boasted waterfall radiator grilles with cascades of chrome and retractable headlights, reminiscent of the luxurious Cords. It was indeed a car to lust after.

In 1949, De Soto, like the other divisions of the Chrysler group, modernized its range. The new models tried out the pontoon style, but the family resemblance remained. The lines were still heavy and massive, and preserved some nostalgic traces of the thirties. The taillights remained clearly detached from the body and although it was too early to talk of fins, the rear fenders finished in two small chrome crests.

Inside was the peaceful and reasonable atmosphere of a tranquil car—no eccentricities, no anomalies. The equipment was pleasant. The round eye of the speedometer was

1949 De Soto Custom

placed right in front of the driver, and four small dials huddled on the left gave the essential information: gasoline level, oil pressure, water temperature and ammeter.

The De Soto's massive engine, with its line of six cylinders and 236 ci created 112 horsepower. It was a reliable engine, a peaceful and robust animal. This unit entered the De Soto family in 1932. Its placid temperament married well with the easygoing character of these cars of modest performance, whose sole ambition was to be the trustworthy servants of a clientele interested only in driving with peace of mind. It was a clientele that also appreciated the semiautomatic transmission, the famous Fluid-Drive, a pure Chrysler product whose strong point is not simplicity, since only two of the four gears are automatic, while the others are manual.

In 1949, De Soto produced 94,203 cars, 3,385 of them ragtops. These modest figures take into account only the new models introduced in the course of the year. At that time, De Soto was gliding through calm waters, far from any excess. Its models, free of all eccentricity, belonged to the things you see every day, without appreciating their qualities.

During the fifties, the De Sotos succumbed to the general delirium and lost their placid temperament. In 1952, they were given a V-8 engine, whose power went through a new ceiling each year. In parallel with this escalation, the style also exploded. Following Chrysler, De Sotos also tried to be terrors of the road. Unfortunately, this frenzy would prove fatal for them.

At the end of the decade, which was marked by a recession, Chrysler, like the other manufacturers, concentrated its efforts on the bottom of the range and launched a compact sedan: the Valiant. But De Soto did not have the means to invest in a study of new models. No matter how often they were altered, the cars would only ever be uglier versions of Chryslers, and in 1961, the make disappeared.

Although they were redesigned in the course of the year, the DeSotos of 1949 remained massive. The vertical bars of the radiator grille earned it the nickname of "rainfall." With its painted metal, encircled dials and chrome-plated ornaments, the interior is typical of the late forties.

1949 Cadillac 62 Series

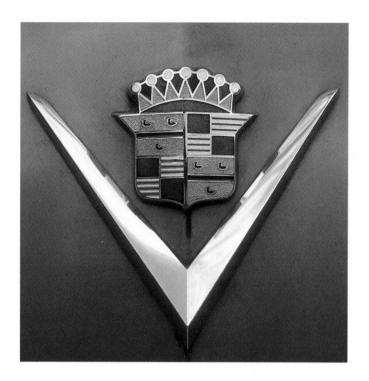

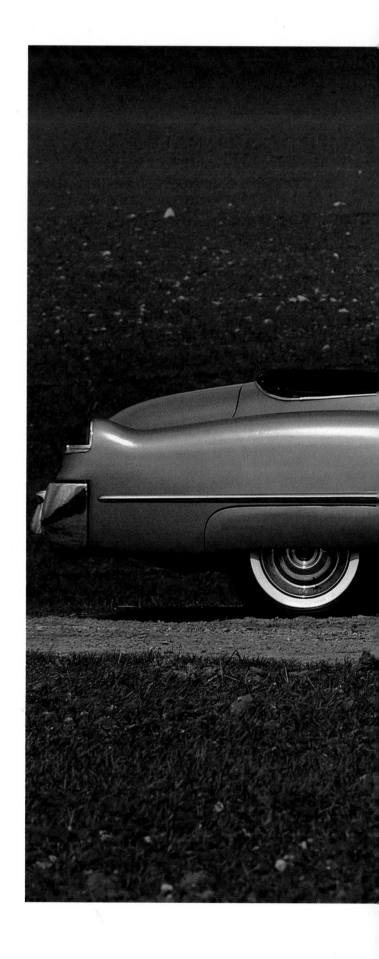

Let the party begin

It was 1939. In the Selfridge military base near Detroit. Harley J. Earl, the great master of style at GM, and some of his collaborators had been authorized to go and see the new fighter aircraft, the Lockheed P-38, even though it was classified top-secret. It was a revelation to them. Earl was fascinated by the elegance of this fighter and its double tail unit. This simple visit would drastically alter the automobile of the fifties; back at the GM Art and Color Center, the designers settled down to their drawing boards. Their mission was to adapt the ideas and aesthetic effects of the P-38 to the automobile.

Thus it was that in 1942, two prototype Cadillacs with fins went around the trial circuits. The war put a temporary stop to these studies, which lay dormant until 1945, but Earl did not give up his plans despite a difficult struggle. The ideas Earl proposed did not always arouse the desired enthusiasm, and the fins themselves did not obtain unanimous approval. Nicholas Dreystadt, Cadillac division general manager was reluctant, and only allowed himself to be

1949 Cadillac
62 Series

swayed by a final sledgehammer argument: with the help of
the aesthetic innovation, Cadillacs would be able to parade
their personality from the radiator grille to the taillights,
whereas the style of American cars generally tended to
collapse weakly beyond the rear window.

The last obstacle was removed and in 1948, Cadillac
unveiled its new models, whose elegance and refinement
contrasted with the heaviness of the preceding models,
dating from 1941. While the eye noticed the two small spurs
at the ends of the rear wings, the overall appearance did not
leave the observer indifferent. The cars were low and lis-
some, adopting a sensible semi-pontoon-line and a generous window surface area. The whole vehicle exuded harmony and elegance, but what neither GM nor Earl could yet
imagine was that these models were going to revolutionize
automobile style in the fifties. The embryo tailfins would
eventually assume crazy proportions, and ten years later
would turn into frightening blades.

Once Cadillac had affirmed its aesthetic identity and
defined its style for the coming decade, it had to provide its
cars with modern mechanics. This was achieved in 1949
with the appearance of a new V-8, designed and developed
from research led by Charles F. Kettering.

Although Kettering held the posts of both vice-president
and technical director of GM, his real passion had always
been for mechanics. In 1910, he perfected coil and distributor ignition—the famous Delco ignition—and two years
later, the electric starter. Fascinated by problems of combus-
tion, he discovered that adding lead to gasoline reduced
pinging in the engine. All his research led him to the con-
clusion that an improvement in performance was depen-
dent on an increase in the compression ratio, for which
engines with side valves would be ill-equipped. On this
basis, he decided in 1936 to start work on a brand-new
engine, using a distribution system with overhead valves. To
compare the two techniques, engineers led by Harry F. Barr
built two engines. The first retained the classic distribution
system; the second used overhead valves. At the end of
November 1941, the two engines were ready for trials, and
the second solution soon took precedence. After World War

In 1949, the fins were already in place. With their
supple silhouette and their leather seats, the
Cadillacs were both elegant and luxurious. They
were also at the leading edge of progress with
their brand-new 160 horsepower V-8.

1949 Cadillac
62 Series

II, the development of this mechanical system was twice modified.

In this period, Cadillac was working on one engine of 289 ci, with a short stroke and a high compression ratio, and on another, lower-compression engine of 309 ci. When the oil companies announced that the promised high-test gasoline would have an octane rating of 90 instead of 100 as originally planned, the 289 ci engine was abandoned. Then in 1947, when the design team learned that Oldsmobile, which had also received the plans of the Kettering V-8, was developing a 303 ci engine, Cadillac management immediately decided to increase the capacity of its engine to 331 ci, so as to preserve its supremacy within GM.

With a 7.5:1 compression ratio and 160 horsepower, the 331 ci V-8 boasted performance that was hardly superior to its predecessor. But the new engine had potential for development, and without any increase in capacity, it went from 190 horsepower in 1952 to 210 horsepower in 1953, 230 in 1954, 250 in 1955 and even 270 in the Eldorado in 1955. This was the engine used in the 1950 twenty-four-hour race at Le Mans by Briggs Cunningham's two cars. The first, a strictly standard car, was classed tenth, with an average speed of 81.538 mph; the second, with a barchetta body and nicknamed Le Monstre, finished eleventh, despite trouble with the gearbox.

The 1949 Cadillac range consisted of twelve models, priced from $2,788 to $4,839. The novelty of the year was the town coupe, a two-door version without uprights, which repeated the lines of the convertible but had a fixed roof made of steel. On November 25, 1949, one of these models became the millionth Cadillac produced since the make was founded. The convertible was present only in the 62 Series, at a price of $3,442, and Cadillac made 8,000 of them out of a total 81,545 cars.

In two years, Cadillac had masterfully laid the foundations of American automobile style for the next ten years and the foundations of engineering for the next quarter century. GM's prestige make was ready; the great party of the fifties could begin.

Although Packard was still in front of Cadillac in 1949, the prestigious GM company won a decisive advantage with cars that were decidedly modern. Compared with the competition, the clear and complete instrumentation indicated that aesthetic aims were being pursued.

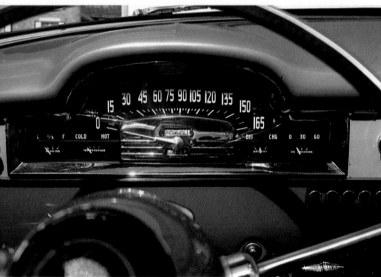

1950 Buick Super Eight

All teeth bared

There are those who swear by Cadillacs, those who revere Packards and those who are fascinated by the Buicks of 1950. No other manufacturer has ever dared to produce a radiator grille with such a grin, a gaping mouth revealing nine dazzling, deadly teeth ready to tear at anything that comes within reach.

Having been entirely redesigned in 1949, the Buicks were once again completely remodeled in 1950. The house style could be spotted a long way off, since the cars preserved traces of the Y-Job, a show car thought up and designed by Harley J. Earl and presented as far back as 1938. The pontoon line was of course adopted, but without excess, and the sides still clearly suggested the shape of the front and rear fenders.

Then there was that radiator grille, that frightening jaw, that terrible grin that Tex Avery could well have used in his cartoons. This "million dollar smile" concealed 4,000 lb. of indestructible cast iron and steel. Unfortunately, it was

1950 Buick Super Eight

abandoned in 1951 because of the high tooling cost, each of its nine teeth being different.

Among the other characteristic gimmicks was the mascot, positioned like a figurehead and above all, the portholes in the sides of the hood.

These Ventiports, as Buick dubbed them, have a story to them. In 1948, Ned Nickles, in charge of design, decided to personalize his Roadmaster ragtop. He cut small holes on either side of the hood, into which he inserted bulbs that were connected directly to the distributor. In this way, there would be a flash with each ignition cycle, giving the impression of an ultrapowerful engine, spitting flames out of its exhausts. Harlow H. Curtice, then president of Buick, was greatly taken by the idea and asked for it to be applied to the company's forty-nine models, but without the lights. To begin with, these portholes provided ventilation for the engine, but they quickly became mere ornaments. For many years, they were a distinctive mark of Buick cars, and they were still to be found, admittedly in a stylized form, on some models from the late seventies.

The convertible presented here, costing $2,476, joined the hunt along with Mercury and De Soto. It belongs to the mid-range Super series, being built on the shortest wheelbase (121.3 inches) and equipped with an intermediate engine, an in-line eight (although with overhead valves) of 263 ci, which peacefully exerts its 124 horsepower when you push the accelerator to the floor. This engine dates from the thirties, but it nevertheless has a solid reputation, making you forget the age of its arteries.

This Buick has many other trumps in its hand. It has helical spring suspension, an original technique already adopted before World War II and one going against the consensus surrounding semi-elliptic plates. Above all, it has the famous Dynaflow gearbox. Models equipped with Dynaflow are marked accordingly on the rear fender, as here. Making its appearance in 1948 and essentially the work of engineer Oliver K. Kelly, this automatic transmission is a pure Buick product that should not be confused with the Hydra-matic, developed by GM for Cadillac, Oldsmobile and Pontiac cars. It functions with exquisite smoothness, and although some reproached its slowness, customers gave it a good reception. In 1954, eighty-five percent of Buicks were equipped with it.

Advancing with measured, confident steps, Buick broke all its records in 1950 and produced 552,827 cars, thereby putting itself in fourth position in the market, behind Chevrolet, Ford and Plymouth. This result was all the more remarkable since the three other manufacturers were making popular models, whereas Buick was aiming its cars at a more demanding clientele. The manufacturer therefore started the fifties in all serenity, but history would blow hot and cold over the Flint firm during the coming decade.

This radiator grille is probably one of the most frightening ever designed. By comparison, the design of the rear is much more peaceful. The pearly reflections of the speedometer glisten directly in front of the driver.

1950 Hudson Commodore Eight

The spirit of independence

Who remembers Hudson? The Step-down line? The fabulous Hornets? Not many, to tell the truth. Admittedly, to find
traces of this independent manufacturer, it is necessary to
search through the dusty drawers of history. However, this
company did have its moment of glory and at one time
enjoyed a fine reputation, being regularly placed among the
five leaders and even producing up to 300,000 cars in 1929!
But the Great Depression was nearly fatal for it, and the firm
owed its salvation only to its derived makes, the Essex and
the Terraplane.

Thanks to weapons orders from the government, Hudson
recovered its financial health during World War II, and in
1948, it presented new models. In the euphoria of the return
to peacetime, the independent manufacturers were the first
to react and offer their customers something other than
those "vaguely reheated prewar spuds," to paraphrase one
American journalist. Of all of them, Hudson was probably
the most daring.

1950 Hudson Commodore Eight

Hudson's team of designers, led by Frank Spring, produced an integral pontoon look that was bolder still than the pontoon styles of Kaiser and Studebaker. With their raised beltline molding, their lowered roofs and their narrow windows, the new Hudsons introduced the Step-down line and were distinguished by an overall height considerably lower than that of the competition. Passengers did not have to squeeze their heads between their knees, however, since the interior space was cleverly enlarged in all dimensions. In fact, it was still possible to get into a Hudson without taking off your hat. The engine was moved forward in its compartment, the rear seat was placed before the axle instead of above it and the floor was lowered as far as possible.

The Company's engineers were able to take advantage of uni-body construction, replacing the classic chassis with a sort of metal cage, which was then covered with the various parts of the body. The lowering of the floor, for example, was made possible by moving the lower side frames that go outside the rear wheels as far apart as possible. Hence that slightly bulbous appearance, reminiscent of the "upturned bathtub" look of Packards from the same year.

In brief, the new Hudsons conspicuously displayed their differences, but their unusual appearance was not uniquely destined to surprise. Thanks to their considerably lowered center of gravity and the rigidity achieved by their construction, these cars were easy to maneuver, agile and reliable; they held the road as stubbornly as an obstinate leech and could get the better of most of their competitors, however winding the course.

To make the best use of all these qualities, Hudson also offered a brand-new engine. But, whereas many manufacturers were busying themselves around V-8s with overhead valves, Hudson unveiled an in-line six with side valves! This mechanical system surprised a few people: it was the largest and most powerful six-cylinder engine in American production, and with 262 ci and 121 horsepower, it was practically evenly matched with the firm's in-line eight-cylinder engine, which dated from 1932 and whose 254.5 ci put out 128 horsepower.

Despite their qualities, the new Hudsons had one huge fault: their uni-body construction did not facilitate restyling, the importance of which is well-known in the United States. The 1950 Hudsons were thus almost identical to earlier Hudsons, and already seemed old-fashioned when compared with the novelties presented by GM. After the regular progress of previous years—92,038 cars in 1947, 117,200 in 1948 and 159,100 in 1949—production fell to 121,408 units in 1950 and Hudson dropped to thirteenth place, despite the

After the war, Hudson was one of the first to adopt the overall pontoon line. In 1950, the Commodore Eight convertible was the most expensive and most luxurious model in the range. It had a hydraulically controlled top and windows. The bar with its crystal glasses was an accessory.

1950 Hudson Commodore Eight

introduction of the new Pacemakers, which were attempting to make a breakthrough as intermediate models.

The large models were the main subjects of this decline; the Commodore Eight series to which this convertible belongs, fell from 28,687 units in 1949 to only 16,731 in 1950. Built on the 124 inch wheelbase, this was also the heaviest model—its well-reinforced metal frame provided it with above-average rigidity—and at $2,893, it was the most expensive in the range. Lovers of convertibles also could choose between the Pacemaker and the Pacemaker Deluxe with a 119 inch wheelbase, or the Super Six and the Commodore Six with a 124 inch wheelbase, all equipped with six-cylinder engines of varying power, whereas the Commodore Eight convertible still contained the old in-line eight-cylinder engine with its 128 horsepower.

Production of the Commodore Eight ragtop remained limited. Hudson made 425 for its total in 1950, lower than the 595 built in 1949. The catalog offered a choice between eight standard colors; four special and four two-tone. The electric top and hydraulically operated windows were delivered as standard (these were offered only as an option on other convertibles).

In 1951, Hudson inserted a new series between the Commodore Six and Eight: the Hornet. Though its style remained identical, this new model introduced an improved version of the six-cylinder engine. Its capacity was brought up to 308 ci, its strength to 145 horsepower. This engine was to eclipse the supremacy of the Oldsmobile Rocket 88 in racing and win the NASCAR championships, from 1952 to 1954.

The new Hornets brought a spurt to production, which rose to 131,915 cars in 1951. But Hudson did not have the means to keep up with the rate imposed by the three big names. To cap its misfortune, the company devoted its last forces to a study of a compact car, as did Nash and Kaiser. But Hudson's customers were not ready for these cars, which attracted only a few eccentrics. This mistake completed the firm's suffocation, and Hudson fell into inexorable decline.

In 1954, Hudson linked its fate to that of Nash to form American Motors. But instead of regaining its strength, Hudson lost its identity. The firm fell into oblivion in 1957, after forty-eight years of existence.

The design of this Hudson is not unlike that of the Packards. The two-tone color scheme lightens the line, and the flow of the chrome-plated trim emphasizes the profile of the car. In 1950, this dashboard looked old-fashioned, since some manufacturers had already abandoned absolute symmetry.

1951 Chevrolet Styleline

Popular elegance

The new Chevy kept everyone waiting. Although rivals Ford and Plymouth had abandoned their prewar models several months earlier, Chevrolet enthusiasts had to be patient and content themselves with cars whose lines, dating from 1942, starkly showed their age. Finally, in January 1949, both customers and dealers heaved a sigh of relief; the leading manufacturer in America—and in the world!—unveiled its new range.

Once again, Chevrolet distinguished itself with cars whose elegance attracted all onlookers. A journalist at the Waldorf Astoria on the day of presentation even said the car resembled a small Cadillac! What could be more pleasing for the great masses of Americans? They would be able to drive a car that had been compared to the best and most prestigious! This was one of Chevrolet's secrets: it always knew how to dazzle its customers with harmonious and pleasing lines.

Compared with the Fords and the Plymouths, the new Chevys were less bulky and less squat, which gave them a

1951 Chevrolet Styleline

great commercial advantage, even though as a whole they offered nothing more than their competitors. Ford could even boast that it offered a V-8 with overhead valves, while Chevrolet had nothing better to propose than its old six-cylinder engine, the Cast Iron Wonder, with its 216.5 ci and 90 horsepower, practically unchanged since 1942.

Owing to Ed Glowacke, head of design at Chevrolet, the new line offered two body variations: the Styleline had a classic trunk; the Fleetline had a fastback rear, similar to the rear ends of the Buick and Cadillac coupes, and was nick-named a sedanet. Customers were not sensitive to the original-ity of these lines, however, and the models were aban-doned in 1953.

Having joined the race for renewal a little late, Chevrolet lost first place to Ford in 1949. To attract more customers and to re-establish its supremacy, it introduced two novelties in 1950. The first was a new hardtop coupe called the Bel Air, which met with huge success. There was a family spirit at GM; this elegant model was directly inspired by the Cadillac De Ville and Oldsmobile Holiday coupes, brought out the previous year. The second novelty was of a technical charac-ter: the Powerglide automatic transmission, a two-speed box developed by Chevrolet and representing a big first in the popular sedan category. With these two innovations, Chev-rolet displayed its vitality on both aesthetic and technologi-cal levels. As a result, it established a new sales record, reaching nearly 1½ million vehicles and considerably out-distancing Ford, which sold 1,208,912 cars.

On the mechanical level, Chevrolets remained economi-cally weak. The Powerglide transmission required a more powerful engine, but engineer Ed Kelley solved the problem by simply taking an engine block from the truck range: 235.5 ci in-line-six that produced 105 horsepower. Models with manual gearshift kept the old engine, whose strength was increased after supreme effort from 90 to 92 horsepower. This old servant would continue to work within the Chev-rolet ranks until 1952, and the 235.5 ci engine would stand in until 1955—the year of the small-block V-8. It would even have the honor of equipping the first Corvettes!

In 1951, Chevrolet paused. The firm still offered its two ranges, Styleline and Fleetline, which were presented in two different versions: Special and DeLuxe. The most represen-tative and exclusive was the Styleline DeLuxe series, which offered the only Chevrolet convertible of the year.

Although GM once again outclassed its eternal rival in 1951 (1,229,986 cars compared with Ford's 1,013,381), cus-tomers were more sensitive to the attractions of the convert-ible offered by Ford; Dearborn delivered 40,934 softtops, whereas Chevrolet convertibles attracted only 20,172 buy-ers. The difference in price ($1,949 for the Ford compared with $2,030 for the Chevrolet) is too minimal to explain this gap. From the point of view of pure power, the six-cylinder Chevrolet engine did better than the Ford V-8 (105 horse-power instead of only 100 horsepower), but as far as attrac-tiveness was concerned the Chevy was clearly left behind and customers noticed the difference.

Dearborn's superiority here was part of the logical course of history, and Chevrolet was forced to take note of it: Ford's convertibles attracted more customers. Neither the Bel Airs of 1955-57—which were nevertheless reputed for their elegance—nor the Corvettes could reverse this trend. But this advantage was only a meager consolation for Ford, which would no doubt have preferred to be number one in all departments.

Thanks to its elegant cars, Chevrolet won a clear advantage over Ford in 1950. Although they were ordinary sedans, the interior presentation was not neglected.

1951 Studebaker Champion

Boldness of the pioneer

You *can* be ninety-nine years old and be in perfect form! This was true of Studebaker in 1951. Before World War II, however, the doyen of South Bend, Indiana, went through a series of ups and downs, plunging into some dizzying abysses and then righting itself at the last moment. For more than ten years, its production was on a roller coaster, falling from 123,216 units in 1930 to 12,531 in 1933, then climbing to 98,000 in 1937, before falling again to 46,787 in 1937, and then finally staging a spectacular recovery.

After the war, Studebaker took its place at the starting block. South Bend outstripped everyone, and the new models that appeared in 1947 left the competition ten years behind. Thanks to those models, the pontoon line made a sensational entrance into the American automobile industry. This bold style is owed to Raymond Loewy. Unlike Harley J. Earl, who put his talent exclusively in the service of the automobile, Loewy practiced his art in all the sectors opened up to him by industry, designing with equal degrees of success teacups, locomotives, photocopiers and refrigera-

1951 Studebaker Champion

Designers have often taken inspiration from airplanes—witness the "bullet nose" of the Studebakers of 1950 and 1951, dreamed up by Raymond Loewy. The instrumentation unit is arranged in an arc around the clock which is centered in the axis of the steering wheel.

tors. He also manifested a fierce desire to preserve his independence, and never attached himself to one single firm.

Loewy's first contacts with the automobile world date back to 1932, when he was approached by Hupmobile. But it was with Studebaker that Loewy maintained the most fruitful and durable relation. It all began when Paul G. Hoffmann, marketing vice-president, requested Loewy's services in designing the 1937 models. With their wind-cutting radiator grilles and their headlights that were semi-integrated into the fenders, they were attractive and sold well.

The models launched in 1947 were thus the second to carry the signature of the Loewy Studio. Their creation caused an argument, however: Virgil Exner also claimed to be responsible for them. After leaving Pontiac in 1939, Exner had joined Loewy's team, and Loewy had confided to him the first studies for the future Studebakers. But the two men could not get along and eventually had gone their separate ways. Ray Cole, chief engineer at Studebaker, more or less provoked the break and took Exner's side, asking him to make alterations to Loewy's designs. With a few pencil strokes, Exner thus modified the front and redesigned the radiator grille. (It is even said that Cole gave Loewy inaccurate plans; at the least, the atmosphere was apparently somewhat unpleasant.)

Finally in 1950, Loewy reassumed total control over Studebaker styling. The front was once again radically modified and all Studebakers got the famous bullet nose, like the front of an airplane without the propeller, which can be spotted from a distance and has the honor of being one of the most unusual radiator grilles.

This period was characterized by more than turmoil in the styling department; Studebaker also scored points on the technological level. In the mid-fifties, the firm launched an automatic gearbox developed in collaboration with Borg-Warner. Along with Packard's Ultramatic, it was the only

1951 Studebaker Champion

automatic transmission system produced by an independent manufacturer. Then in 1951, the V-8 with overhead valves appeared. With 232 ci and 120 horsepower, it was not of the same caliber as the engines produced by GM or Chrysler, but it did bring in a fashion for compact V-8s of less than 300 ci, to which Dodge, Plymouth, Ford and Chevrolet would later convert. This brand-new mechanical system was installed in the Commanders, while the Champions continued to be served by the old six-cylinder engine, a peaceful beast whose 169 ci produced a modest 85 horsepower.

For the time, Studebaker offered a fine spectrum of versions: thirteen Champion models and eight Commanders, with a wide choice of bodies. The most original of all was unquestionably the five-seater coupe, whose rear consisted of four windows arranged in a rotunda shape; detractors said you couldn't tell the front from the back! Each of the two ranges included a convertible: the Regal Commander and the State Champion. At $2,157 and $2,381, these were the most expensive models in their respective series.

Anyone yearning for the pleasures of the open air had to be quick—in 1952, the manufacturer included the two convertibles in its catalog for the last time. These ragtops underwent the same alterations as those applied to the whole range. The bullet nose disappeared in favor of a more conventional radiator grille, equipped with teeth that were meant to be aggressive and that stretched along the whole width of the car. As for the two engines, they remained unchanged and compared with the opposition, appeared increasingly weak.

Studebaker was preoccupied with other things. The firm was making feverish preparations for the 1953 vintage. Once more owing to Loewy's pencil, the elegance of the future models was to amaze all of America. Unfortunately, Studebaker had more difficulty assuming its independence. The gulf between the three big manufacturers and the others increased by the day.

Studebaker got through the fifties with the help of the banks and in 1959, with the launch of the little Lark, it even staged a temporary return to health. Nevertheless, this comeback was not sufficient to save the company.

While the Studebaker Commander was equipped with a modern V-8, the Champion had to make do with an in-line six engine of modest performance. In 1953, the ragtops were to disappear from the Studebaker catalog.

1953 Cadillac Eldorado

Wheels of fortune

Like the fairy tale horses who changed sand on the road into gold dust with their hooves, the Cadillac Eldorado stirred up and left in its wake a cloud in which the splendor and brilliance of the American Dream glistened for all to see.

In a sense, this sumptuous convertible represents Cadillac's masterpiece. Having skillfully imposed its style in 1948, the firm took a permanent place at the top of the Detroit hierarchy and became the symbol of luxury and riches—to the detriment of Packard, which was caught up in its traditions and was dealt its final blow when the Eldorado made its appearance.

Eldorado . . . The very name evokes an inaccessible paradise, a country of immeasurable treasures where the poorest of the poor can, without the least effort, become incredibly rich. The most surprising thing is that this name was not the result of extensive research, nor of long debates. Cadillac, which organized an internal competition, owes it to a secretary in the commercial department!

1953 Cadillac Eldorado

The Cadillac Eldorado was a real dream car, descended into the streets. It may be recognized by the curves at the doors, its spoked wheels and, above all, its wraparound windshield, the first to make an appearance in a standard car. The cockpit offered a degree of luxury that was unprecedented at the time.

Although it was built on the same 126 inch wheelbase as the 62 Series, the Eldorado was nevertheless a unique model in the range. Indeed, it had several distinctive features that underlined its differences: a lowered chassis; a beltline molding that curved at the doors; and a sheet metal top that continued the profile of the trunk, extending and refining its lines. But the most tangible mark of the Eldorado's exceptional character was its wraparound windshield; the Eldorado was the first standard car to be equipped with one of these, although the entire American car industry, not just GM, would soon follow suit. As a last touch, the car sported superb spoked wheels, also available as an option on other models.

On the other hand, Cadillac retained the rear end design, with its characteristic fins, and the radiator grille from the 62 Series. This radiator grille provoked Harley Earl's anger. He wanted to redesign the fenders in the form of a crosier by including the enormous buffers, the famous Dagmars. When his proposal was rejected, Earl became piqued and took his sketches to Oldsmobile. In 1954, however, Cadillac gave in to the Great Master's wishes.

Mechanically, the Eldorado was a replica of other Cadillacs. Its V-8, directly derived from the 1949 engine with overhead valves, was a 331 ci, producing 210 horsepower at 4150 rpm. This was originally coupled to a GM Hydra-matic gearbox. On August 12, 1953, however, the Livonia factory where these gearboxes were produced was destroyed by fire. The Cadillacs were then quickly modified to accommodate the Buicks' Dynaflow gearbox. A total of 28,600 cars were

equipped in this way, and it is probable that a certain number of Eldorados suffered the same fate.

In the end, 532 Eldorado dreamboats, as they were called, were produced in 1953. Not many compared with the 109,651 Cadillacs that left the factory that year, but a considerable number for a car that cost $7,750! The Eldorado was $3,500 more than a ragtop from the 62 Series and fully deserved the title of Solid-Gold Cadillac—but nothing was too expensive for the American jet set, who snapped up anything that glittered and that could provide a dazzling symbol of their success.

Cadillac could partly justify this sum by the hyperluxurious equipment. There was, for example, complete leather upholstery, available in four colors and set off by numerous chrome ornaments. There was also a special dashboard, covered with leather, whose design was continued on the doors. Finally, there were electrically controlled seats, windows and hood; power steering; radio with automatic tuning; and dual heaters—all fairly uncommon equipment in 1953 and included with the intention of providing exceptional comfort for the passengers.

Mere figures aside, the Eldorado was a remarkable banner for Cadillac. But in 1953, all of GM decided to fight. Buick and Oldsmobile also put forward their special models, with the former producing the Skylark, the latter the Fiesta. These two magnificent convertibles, produced on a limited scale of 1,690 and 458 cars, respectively, were superbly presented and intended to enhance the other models. GM was indeed number one; it had the know-how and knew how to make itself known.

1953 Packard Caribbean

The weight of tradition

In 1953, Warner Brothers organized a big competition to find a stage name for the young actress Joan Weldon (whose career turned out to be a short one). The first prize was to be the brand-new Packard Carribean cabriolet, presented as the most prestigious American sports car! This anecdote shows to what extent the name of this make was surrounded by an aura of magic in the early fifties.

Unfortunately, the reality was much gloomier: Packard was fighting tooth and nail for its survival.

The East Grand Boulevard manufacturers had bungled their entry into the fifties and missed the start of the great technological competition initiated by Cadillac and Oldsmobile in 1949. With the exception of the excellent Ultramatic gearbox, presented in 1950, the firm had produced no more innovations for some time. Pinned to the spot by the competition, Packard had first to parry as quickly as possible. It was faced with one priority: the production of a new and more seductive line. The work was entrusted to a young designer, John Reinhart, who later distinguished himself at Lincoln by designing the sublime Continental Mark II.

1953 Packard Caribbean

The new Packard range was unveiled in March 1951. The result was hardly a dazzling success. Packard had contented itself with adopting the current norms, without adding the slightest hint of originality nor the smallest personal touch. The thick-lipped radiator grille did not arouse a storm of applause either. Packard's hopes were disappointed, and at the end of 1951, the firm found itself with nearly 30,000 unsold cars.

Conscious of its weaknesses and of being left behind, management had meanwhile decided to appeal to a savior. The man of providence was James J. Nance, who had already achieved miracles in domestic appliances, and he accepted, without being pressed, the lucrative offer made to him to take charge of Packard's destiny.

Radical measures were necessary to put the firm back on the rails, and Nance launched a vast program of modernization, which included—finally—starting work on a V-8 intended for 1954. In the meantime, customers had to be kept happy. Therefore, once again, Packard heated up the leftovers, which mainly dated from the forties!

In 1953, numbered identifications of 200, 300 and 400 disappeared in favor of more evocative names. Thus the Mayfair and the Cavalier appeared, joining the Patrician, while the Clippers formed the whole of the low range. But the real novelty of the year was the Caribbean, a luxury convertible in direct competition with the Cadillac Eldorado.

Like its GM rival, the Caribbean was essentially a response to the needs of promotion. Its exceptional character was intended to energize and rejuvenate Packard's image. Closely derived from the standard ragtop, the Caribbean also borrowed some aesthetic ideas from the Pan American, a show car that had been presented at the New York Car Show in 1952 and from which Richard Teague, the designer in charge of the Caribbean operation, took his inspiration. This convertible was distinguished by its open rear fenders, which revealed superb spoked wheels struck with the famous red hexagon, and by the wide chrome trim emphasizing the wheelhousings and the bottom of the body. At the front, the hood was surmounted by a wide air intake; at the back, the car sported a Continental kit, and a tapered plate closed over each of the two taillights. But the most striking feature of the Caribbean was the purity of its lines, free of all ornaments, smooth as lacquer, standing out against their flamboyant surroundings.

The Packard Caribbean is the equivalent of the Cadillac Eldorado, a special model in the range. The rear sports two small chrome-plated crests above the lights and a Continental kit. Note the quality of the paint work and chrome on this Californian model.

1953 Packard Caribbean

Many preferred the curves of the Eldorado, where the line of the fenders extends beneath the lines of the top and the windows, but the Packard demands respect with its dignified and sober appearance—a sobriety that is repeated in the interior. A simply painted dashboard made of sheet metal, instrumentation entrusted to three dials grouped together on a metal panel and a chrome-plated loudspeaker surmounted by the radio—this is what the driver finds behind the immense ivory steering wheel. Amid the frenzy that was gradually taking hold of car maufacturers, the old lady of Detroit preserved a certain degree of rigor.

Packard asked for one more effort from its faithful in-line eight engine with five bearings and 327 ci, from which it extracted 180 horsepower. This was not so bad compared with the 180 and 188 horsepower of the Chrysler and Buick V-8s, since only Lincoln and Cadillac beat the 200 horsepower barrier that year. But in 1954, to keep itself in the race, Packard would be obliged to recall its big engine, which had been improved in 1951. Without regard for its venerable age, this ancestor from the thirties was rebored, its stroke was shortened and its compression ratio was pushed to the limits of apoplexy. Packard finally wrung 212 horsepower from the 359 ci of this faithful, devoted and astonishingly adaptable servant.

Taking its exclusive character into account, the Caribbean may be considered a success. Seven hundred fifty cars were sold at a price of $5,210 each, which is not excessive if you consider that a basic Clipper cost as much as $2,500. Furthermore, the overall balance sheet for 1953 was fairly encouraging, since the firm produced more than 90,000 vehicles.

Unfortunately, the revival expected in 1954 did not take place, and the new Packards with their V-8 engines did not appear until 1955. In the interval, Nance, who knew that the survival of small manufacturers was threatened, attempted to form a fourth automobile company by grouping together the independent firms. He contacted Nash and Hudson, and finally associated Packard to Studebaker, but this union did not even delay the final day of reckoning.

The sides of the car are of great purity, as is the design of the dashboard. Behind the big ivory steering wheel, the driver finds three circular dials grouped together on a finely worked metal panel, while the central part is occupied solely by the radio.

1954 Chevrolet Corvette

Feline car

American cars are commonly described as flashy, non-chalant monsters—disproportionate and debonair. The Corvette provides a scathing reply to these simplistic cliches.

In the early fifties, the Nash Healey and Kaiser Darrin came into being, and the West Coast saw the appearance of the first manufacturers of polyester (a material created during the war) kits, who offered original bodies that were adaptable to mass-produced chassis. But all these initiatives did not appear to move Detroit, where the main maufacturers continued to produce big family sedans, spacious and comfortable, satisfying the good people. The figures prove them right: in 1952, of four million vehicles sold in the United States, only 11,000 were sports cars—hardly 0.3 percent of the market! Still, the fantasy of the wild and powerful roadster slumbered in the heart of the design studios. The people who designed Chevrolets, Fords and Plymouths all nursed, whether secretly or not, a desire to create a car that could live up to their great passion.

1954 Chevrolet Corvette

Harley J. Earl found a way to make his ideas concrete. Thanks to the motoramas, where GM exhibited its dream cars, Earl had a tremendous outlet for his fertile imagination. His first dream car dated from 1938. It was the Buick Y–Job, which already appeared in the form of a two-door, two-seater cabriolet.

After the war, Earl went back to the studies that were so dear to him. In 1951, he presented the Le Sabre and the following year, the Buick XP 300, which brought together the ingredients of a real sports car: reduced ground clearance, extended silhouette, two-seater cockpit and high-level performance. But Earl had other ideas in his head. Apart from these futurist features, he wanted to create a small roadster that could be mass-produced. In the fall of 1951, he started work, and for help he turned to a young engineer: Robert F. McLean.

In a departure from the usual custom, McLean approached his study from the rear axle and then worked forward, centering the cockpit and the engine compartment. To reduce the manufacturing costs of the future car, Earl asked his collaborators to use and adapt as many massed-produced parts as possible. Ed Cole, an engineer who had recently transferred from Cadillac to Chevrolet, took charge of the operation.

Cole was also to develop the engine. At the time, Chevrolet had only a solid six-cylinder unit, a machine well-suited to family sedans but much too peaceful to power a sports car. However, in less time than it takes to pass the checkered flag, this engine's strength was increased from 106 to 150 horsepower, thanks to a new camshaft, valves operated mechanically instead of hydraulically, a compression ratio increased from 7.5:1 to 8:1, three sidedraft carburetors and some minor adjustments.

The choice of transmission was dictated by simplicity. Since the three-speed mechanical box was too complicated to install, the engineers adopted the automatic two-speed Powerglide transmission system, which could be adapted without difficulty.

In January 1953, the Corvette was unveiled to the public at the Waldorf Astoria Hotel in New York. Harlow Curtice, president of GM, and Thomas Keating, director of Chevrolet, had known of its existence from the middle of 1952, but they were waiting for the verdict of this great premiere before giving the green light to the car's production. About four million visitors saw the car, and enthusiasm was almost unanimous. The Corvette would finally be able to take to the streets.

Six months later, on June 30, 1953, the production line got under way in premises adjacent to the Chevrolet factory. Start-up was laborious. The problems stemmed from assembling body elements in fiberglass, a material chosen partly for its lightness, but mainly to avoid the manufacture of pressing tools and thereby save time and money. Unfortunately, fiberglass was still new and its use had not yet been completely mastered.

Rather than put imperfect cars on the market, Chevrolet decided to halt production voluntarily and to refuse firm orders for the time being. In total, only 300 Corvettes were produced in 1953, constituting a pre-series that familiarized staff with new work methods. The only color was Polo White with a Sportsman Red interior. Not having to worry about combining different colors, the workers could concentrate on assembling the parts.

One thing is certain: the Corvette did not correspond to the current norms at Detroit. Short and feline, it seemed rather bare. The absence of certain features was in fact surprising. For example, the doors did not have outside handles—to open them, you had to lean inside!—and the side windows were simple flaps hung from the top. On the other hand, the cockpit was comfortable and well-produced. The dashboard was harmonious and the instrumentation was complete. Behind the seats, the top was swallowed up by a hatch, and when uncovered, the car was still more elegant. Finally, the trunk was particularly large for a sports car.

The customers, worried by teething problems, hesitated. While a monthly rate of 1,000 cars had been planned for 1954, Chevrolet delivered only 3,640 Corvettes in one year and found itself with 1,500 cars left over. Some initial faults had, however, been corrected. The attachment for the top and the arrangement of the control units had been improved, as had the insulation of the electric circuit; the Blue Flame Six engine had gained another five horsepower thanks to a new camshaft; and the buyer now had a choice among five different colors. Above all, the assembly problems had been solved.

None of this made any difference. Customers continued to shun the car, and at GM's nerve center, some directors were turning their backs on it. The Corvette's career risked being cut short after only a year and a half of existence.

The Chevrolet Corvette, which appeared in 1953, was the first standard American roadster. Its short, feline body was made from fiberglass. The car looks good with the spoked wheels, although they are not original. The dashboard has often been criticized because you have to rely on the passenger to read the dials on the right.

1955 Cadillac 62 Series

Just say "Cadillac"

Cadillac—the name rolls off the tongue and evokes, all on its own, the miracle of Uncle Sam. In 1955, the models ostentatiously projected their radiator grilles, and paraded their opulent curves as provocatively as did Marilyn Monroe. The small fins were still present and still inoffensive, but the Eldorado was already sharpening its own in preparation for great years to come.

Well-to-do customers were wild about these large candies and their colors as tender as an Elvis Presley love song. As they glided down from Beverly Hills, they liked to settle in the soft leather of the wide seats and watch the world through the distorting curves of the wraparound windshield. With one finger, they could open the top and lower the electric windows; with one hand movement, they could start the air conditioning. With their elbows leaning on the car doors, they let themselves be carried along by the silky sound of the 331 ci V-8, created in 1949, with its 250 to 270 horsepower. The driver could also sample the voluptuous pleasures of the automatic transmission, power steering and

1955 Cadillac
62 Series

brakes delivered as standard on all the models, which could be driven with the finger tips and whose two tons of chrome and steel were balanced on a supple suspension.

In the euphoria of 1955, Cadillac sold more than 140,000 cars and took twelfth place in the market—a position it was to keep in 1956 but would not achieve again until 1969! The Cadillacs of the mid-fifties could in any case cruise along in peace. The competition was moribund, like Packard, or exhausted from trying to keep up, like Lincoln and Imperial.

Harley J. Earl, GM's great designer, imposed his style and made relentless efforts to stimulate the covetousness of his customers. In 1955, he finished preparing the Eldorado Brougham, a sumptuous four-door sedan without uprights and with a stainless steel roof, which concealed numerous refined and extravagant tricks, such as the glove compartment containing six crystal glasses with magnetic bases, or the armrest containing a perfume atomizer. Presented as a show car in 1956, this car was to be marketed in 1957 at the stunning price of $13,000—and it was claimed that Cadillac lost $10,000 on each model sold!

The 1955 convertible cost $4,448, $1,838 less than the Eldorado of the same year. With production of 8,150 and 3,950, respectively, the two cars offered customers a sign that they belonged to a certain elite group.

If, after this, you are still not convinced of the exclusive character of the Cadillacs, ponder this: the great restaurants and luxury hotels used to reserve private parking lots for them!

Classy customers went wild about these big, delicately colored candies and drove proudly around on the leather seats, listening to Elvis ballads. It was during the fifties that Cadillac definitively established its supremacy, with cars of personal design and ultra-luxurious equipment.

1956 Buick Roadmaster

Descent into hell

The name Roadmaster says it all. A Buick is made to dominate the roads. It is an indefatigable mount, eating up milestones as effectively as a lumberman brings down a 100 year old oak.

In 1953, Buick had equipped itself with a V–8. In itself, this was not a real innovation, because many manufacturers had already built V–8s. But the engine had some distinctive features. First of all, it was the first V–8 to be equipped with twelve volts. Second, Joseph D. Turlay, the creator of the engine, had resolutely opted for a short stroke. Although they did not offer the greatest power, the Buicks equipped in this way had nothing to fear from anyone, not even from the dreaded Chrysler 300s, with whom they successfully crossed swords in competition. Having 322 ci and 164 horsepower from the start, this engine achieved 255 horsepower on the Roadmaster ragtop of 1956, which could shoot from 0 to 60 mph in less than ten seconds and could reach speeds of up to 112 mph. This performance was displayed on the Red-liner speedometer, a subtle piece of equipment dreamed up

1956 Buick Roadmaster

by the engineer, Helgeby, from the AC Spark Plug division, inaugurated in 1954, and which replaced the traditional needle with a red line which grew longer as the speed increased.

In standard production, the engine was coupled to the Dynaflow gearbox, which had been greatly improved since its first appearance. The Dynaflow guaranteed more powerful acceleration, commensurate with the ambitions of the car. This transmission was also used in the Supers and the Century, while the Specials could have it as an option.

While 1953 was marked by mechanical renewal, 1954 was the year of overall restyling. Buick adopted a GM specialty: the wraparound windshield. The sides, which were now perfectly smooth, sported a V-shaped chrome molding, which evoked the movement of the fenders at the front and the rear, the latter ending in embryonic fins. All this was to become refined over the years and in 1956, the Buicks were elegant thoroughbred cars, particularly the Supers and the Roadmasters, built on a 127 inch wheelbase, while the Specials and Centurys were five inches shorter. The vertical bars of the radiator grille had been swapped for a finer grille and the rear fender was now no more than a pure, rectilinear fin ending in a vertical light. Finally, the rear wheels were completely exposed, a stylistic effect that lightened the style and was adopted by the whole range that year.

The interior was dominated by the GM atmosphere in all its splendor. The top of the dashboard consisted of stuffing covered in imitation leather, while the bottom was made of painted sheet metal. Between the two, a molding of embossed metal contained the instrumentation, which consisted of rectangular dials, a tendency that was becoming widespread.

Buick went through some euphoric years. In 1954, the firm seized third place in the market from Plymouth, who had occupied it since 1931, and it established a new production record in 1955, with 781,296 cars put into circulation; it was not until 1973 that this figure was exceeded.

But the sky over Flint was not as serene as may have been imagined. For some time, Buicks had been subject to

chronic weaknesses. The rear axles were ill-suited to the power and the brakes faded too often. Ralph Nader mentioned this problem in his indictment, *Unsafe At Any speed*. Buick, while caring too much for quantity, had paid too little attention to quality. But it paid the price, because customers and dealers started to complain more openly. The famous slogan—"When the best car is made, Buick makes it"—had been seriously tarnished. To cap it all, the 1957 line, although it was elegant, was vigorously criticized. Its three-part rear window was reproached with being too old-fashioned and the pronounced tip of the wraparound windshield was criticized for hindering access to the front seats. A California dealer even told his colleagues to buy any old models that were still available, because they were the only marketable ones!

After its years of glory, Buick was embarking on a nightmare. From 1958 to 1961, production fell below the 300,000 level and in 1960, the manufacturer slumped abruptly into ninth place. Ironically, the make, which was renowned for its opulent cars, was to be partly saved by the small Special and Skylark models, appearing on the market in the sixties. Buick would regain its vitality. Although these compact cars may not always find favor in our eyes, let us at least recognize the fact that they saved one of the most engaging makes in Motor City.

Only the America of the fifties knew how to display such provocatively contrasting colors with elegance. The black and pink of this Buick are separated by a chrome-plated molding, whose lines are reminiscent of the design of the fenders. Moleskin padding, wide molding made of embossed metal—the dashboard is typical of GM's style of the period.

1956 Packard Caribbean

The latter-day queen

Nineteen fifty-five was a great year for the American automobile. The fins lost their timidity; the pontoon style, created almost ten years before, was in its prime; the panoramic fender was gaining ground; the lines became more refined. Ford launched the Thunderbird, eleven manufacturers renewed their ranges and four brand-new V-8s made their appearance. But in this feast of novelties, the prize must go to Packard, which in a supreme effort made up the ground it had lost since the beginning of the fifties. Aesthetics in keeping with current tastes, original suspension and above all, an entirely new engine: the 1955 vintage brought together all the ingredients necessary to return the sick bird to health.

Richard Teague, who was particularly inspired, masterfully modernized Packard's lines, which dated from 1951. This facelift was an illusionist's trick. The extended rear fenders ended in cathedral lights similar in style to those of Buick—except on the Clippers, which retained the 1954 rear—and the front was prolonged by visors over the head-

1956 Packard Caribbean

lights. The car thus seemed lower and longer, whereas the beltline molding had not been reduced one inch. Teague also adapted the panoramic fender to the old front end. Finally, the disdainful pout of the radiator grille was changed into a more pleasing smile.

This successful restyling was not the main trump held by the new range, however. In contrast to the classic make-up of contemporary construction, the Packard 55s were equipped with Torsion Level Ride, a revolutionary suspension system with longitudinal torsion bars and an electric headlight leveler. The press unanimously applauded the ingenuity of this system and acclaimed the new Packards' excellent road performance, which rivaled that of the best sports cars of the time.

Above all was the engine—the long-awaited Packard V-8. Modern, high performance and reliable (a Patrician covered 25,000 miles at over 100 mph without loss of power), this engine immediately overtook its competitors. The engineers, who did not do things by halves, aimed for a large cylinder capacity. Thus, the 352 ci engine could produce either 260 or 275 horsepower under the hood of the Caribbean. With the exception of the Chrysler 300, which was intended for racing and whose V-8 offered 300 horsepower, the Caribbean was the most powerful car on the American market. The Clippers received a miniaturized version, making do with 225 or 245 horsepower from 320 ci.

Benefiting from the larger engine—which gave it an advantage of five horsepower over the Eldorado—the Caribbean was brought back to its role of top model. The only ragtop in the catalog, it was also the most expensive model in the range at $5,932, and Packard reserved for it the company's most refined features. The vehicle's occupants were thus spared any unnecessary effort, since the Caribbean was the automated car par excellence, from the electric seats and windows, to the locating of radio stations, to the two antennas atop the rear fenders.

To clearly show how different it was, the Caribbean sported characteristic decoration in three colors. Although lacking in taste, this make-up nevertheless had the advantage of being recognizable from afar. The cars were decked out in a kitsch white-pink-black, corresponding to a delectable vanilla-pistachio-chocolate sundae.

Unfortunately, customers had lost confidence, and to crown it all, the Twin-Ultramatic transmission, which offered a double range of speeds, was not well-suited to the high power of the engine and posed numerous problems. This lack of reliability damaged Packard's image of robustness at the most inopportune moment. With only 55,000 cars sold, 1955 was therefore a failure for Nance, who was aiming at 100,000 vehicles.

In 1956, however, Packard persevered. Some aesthetic alterations were carried out on the bodywork and all the models were given Torsion Level Ride suspension. The Clippers now formed an entirely separate make. As a $52 option, the Ultramatic transmission system could be given button controls, mounted on the right of the steering column.

Somehow, the Caribbean continued its career. In a final surge, its engine leapt to 374 ci, producing 310 horsepower.

Vanilla, pistachio and chocolate—this 1956 Packard Caribbean is an ice-cream sundae on wheels. It was equipped with the largest engine in production: a 374 ci V-8 with 310 horsepower. The metallic dashboard is a piece of modern sculpture.

The car became a formidable beast, achieving the quarter-mile in less than ten seconds and touching 125 mph. Thanks to the suspension, its roadholding capabilities were excellent, and a specialist journal stated that on a winding road, it was possible to maintain astonishingly fast speeds.

Behind the big two-tone steering wheel, the massive but original dashboard—a flashy wall of metal, worked like a modern sculpture—contained a complete range of instruments. Among other signs of riches were reversible cushions, with a leather side for town, a cloth side for the country.

All this was to no avail. The game had been lost for good. Nance's vision of a fourth automobile cartel would remain forever a pipe dream. The alliance with Studebaker was a failure.

In June 1956, the last Packards—perhaps the best ones—left the East Grand Boulevard factory. A total of 276 Caribbean convertibles had been produced, compared with 500 in 1955. These were the last representatives of a dynasty that would later act as a figurehead for a few hybrids produced on a Studebaker base, before disappearing forever.

1956 Chevrolet Bel Air

Mighty Mouse

To fight off boredom on a Saturday night in the sleepy towns of deepest America, the kids of the early fifties held improvised races along the rectangular avenues, acceleration tests at every traffic light. At nightfall, old Fords and souped-up Mercurys gathered at the intersections. But in 1955, the son of the local Chevrolet dealer was king. Thanks to the new Chevy, he sowed terror and ran off with his friends' dates, leaving them green with envy.

Until the mid-fifties, Chevrolets had pursued their destiny with resignation. They were sensible cars, designed with moderation; reliable, robust, hardy and you got into them without emotion. In 1955, the new models brushed their past aside. Those peaceful sedans, intended for quiet fathers, were to become the idols of the young and attract the generation of *Rebel Without a Cause*.

The team of designers, including Clare McKichan, Bob Veryzer, Chuck Stebbins and Carl Renner, followed Harley J. Earl's directives with moderation. With a gentle and relax-

1956 Chevrolet Bel Air

ing silhouette that gives off tranquil harmony, a radiator grille of pure lines, sober fins, discreet red lights and just the right amount of chrome to avoid extravagance, the new Chevys were unlike any other American car.

The engineers, led by Ed Cole, had surpassed themselves in perfecting the long-awaited Chevrolet V-8 (the previous one dated from 1919!). They had been asked for a solid engine that was easy to repair, and they brought out a formidable beast in the small-block. It was to be a landmark. Compared with the competition, it was a small, compact and light unit (lighter than the old six-cylinder engine, which was still available) that turned over like a coffee mill. It made a start with 265 ci, producing 162 horsepower, with the Power Pack pumping out 180 horsepower, thanks to a quad carburetor and double exhaust. Never in the history of the Chevy had such a frisky machine been produced. It was so small and so invigorating that it was nicknamed the Mighty Mouse, a mouse motor that would give rise to the best Chevrolet engines in the years to come.

The manufacturer set the tone by baptizing its new range "The Hot One," and in 1955 an inspired Chevrolet introduced a new version: the Nomad. This was a two-door station wagon, designed in a slender and superb style by Carl Renner. The presence of this model in the range was not absolutely justified, but people did not tire of admiring the elegance of its features. The Nomad blended a utilitarian vehicle with a coupe; the result was a sporty station wagon ahead of its time. It was the most expensive model in the line, and also the classiest; today, it is without a doubt the most sought after.

The year 1955 was an excellent vintage for all the manufacturers, but for Chevrolet it was particularly good. With 1,704,667 cars, the firm flooded the market and on its own accounted for one quarter of the total production! Ford was left a considerable distance behind and consoled itself as best it could with the thought that its T-bird had beaten the Corvette, but this victory was only a grain of sugar in a bitter cup of tea.

In the United States, the law of annual change spares no one. Thus for 1956, Chevrolet put its cars back on the drawing board, although the manufacturer rightly thought the Chevys were still fine cars and could make do with minor adjustments. At the front, the radiator grille now stretched across the entire width of the car and encompassed the turn indicators. The fins were prolonged but remained modest. The hood lost its curves and the decoration of the sides separated the colors in a new, more elegant way. In brief, the purity of the whole was preserved while also being Americanized.

After some teething problems, which were quickly overcome, the V-8 was already showing its fangs. Its basic versions still offered 162 horsepower with the manual gearbox and 170 horsepower with the Powerglide automatic. But the Power Pack now provided 205 horsepower, and Zora Arkus-Duntov, a talented motor mechanic, turned his attention to this. Thanks to a special camshaft, a higher compression ratio and a pair of quad carburetors, the power immediately increased to 225 horsepower. This still hotter version was installed in the Corvettes, which thus became real racers.

Compared with those of its competitors, the lines of this 1956 Bel Air are rather peaceful. But the car is equipped with a powerful V-8 known as the Mighty Mouse. The upholstery repeats the colors of the body and the V-shaped decorations which are also on the dashboard.

The 1956 range offered nineteen versions in all. At the bottom of the scale was the 150 series, largely forgotten, because of its lack of style and sophistication. Then came the 210 series, which was less destitute. Finally, at the top of the pack, was the legendary Bel Air, a popular car that displayed its graces with great success and which the American worker could, for a few extra dollars, embellish with refinements that had been reserved, not so long ago, for the Cadillacs. This was also the car that had the finest bodystyle, such as the Nomad, whose unnecessary splendor attracted 7,886 customers, and the ragtop.

Chevrolet produced 41,268 Bel Airs in 1956—the same, to within a few units, as in 1955. The Ford Sunliners, selling at $2,359 compared with $2,344 for the Chevrolet, were apparently more attractive, since Ford sold 58,147 of them. However, the overall annual balance sheet confirmed Chevrolet's supremacy, and Chevrolet retained first place.

For 1957, the designers turned their hand to these cars one last time. Without touching the central cell, they grafted on some slender fins, while the radiator grille was laden with chrome. But chevrolet was supplanted by Ford, which presented completely new models.

In the United States, more than anywhere else, cars quickly go out of fashion, and Chevrolet actively prepared the new line-up planned for 1958. The future models were to be larger and wider, but also heavier and bulkier in the eyes of purists who had placed the 1955–57 models on a pedestal once and for all. No other Chevy has since been able to make those enthusiasts change their minds.

1957 Oldsmobile Super 88

A passion for innovation

If you ignore its first years of existence, Oldsmobile has a faultless history. Today, it is the oldest American make still in production. In the twenties, however, GM assigned it a thankless role, that of intermediary range intended for the middle classes.

This difficult position did not prevent Oldsmobile from being constantly at the forefront of innovation. In 1937, its cars adopted semi-automatic transmission; in the following year, they were the first to be equipped with the Hydramatic, the famous GM gearbox, a miracle of smoothness. In 1949, a new thunderbolt flashed over Lansing: a few weeks before Cadillac, Oldsmobile presented a brand-new, high-performance V-8 called the Rocket, which could burn the asphalt at traffic lights. The climb toward increased power had started.

The list of innovations did not stop there. The year 1953 was marked by the presentation of the Fiesta, a superluxury convertible in the tradition of the Cadillac Eldorado and Buick Skylark. Then, in 1954, the wraparound windshield

1957 Oldsmobile Super 88

was introduced and the Autronic Eye, a refinement until then reserved only for Cadillacs, was offered as an option.

Oldsmobile got people talking about itself again by presenting several dream cars intended to feed the imaginations of its customers. The first of these was the Starfire, unveiled in 1953. Unlike other contemporary cars, this two-seater convertible, with its plastic body, was not merely the product of dreaming frenzy. On the contrary, its distinct silhouette revealed an immediate future that became reality with the 1957 ragtop. In this car we can also find elegant and sensible curves, forming a long and low profile; a side molding running from the door handle to the end of the rear fenders; and above all, the characteristic radiator grille, a perfect oval, with glittering chrome lips opening around an astonished pout.

Since the appearance of the Futuramic in 1948, Oldsmobile constantly refined its style. The 1957 models, which were among the most beautiful and elegant of the year, revealed a perfect mastery of the pontoon style. Nevertheless, they did not escape the gimmicks, without which an American car would look naked. The headlights were surrounded with chromeplated visors and the taillights looked like laser guns armed for space warfare.

The 1957 range included three series. The Golden Rocket 88 and the Super 88 were built on a short chassis with a 122 inch wheelbase, whereas the Starfire 98 was built on a longer 126 inch wheelbase. Each series offered a ragtop, prices varying between $3,182 and $4,217, with the Super 88 presented here costing $3,447.

Unlike other makes, whose reputations were crumbling away, the Oldsmobiles retained all their qualities and their advantages. Among them, the V-8 Rocket presented a shock factor. Since the early fifties, it had won significant victories in racing—the NASCAR championship from 1949 to 1951 and the Carrera Panamericana in 1950—and Oldsmobiles

were among the terrors of the freeways, closely watched by the police, especially since the specter of speed limits was already beginning to be raised. In 1957, this engine produced 277 horsepower with a cylinder capacity of 371 ci, but a popular option, the Rocket J2, pumped out 300 horsepower with the help of three dual carburetors. Equipped in this fashion, an Oldsmobile could go from 0 to 60 mph in less than eight seconds and could still teach a thing or two to some of the more unruly European sports cars. The Hydramatic enabled this power to be exploited to the fullest, and was probably the most efficient and robust transmission in the entire line of American production.

In 1958, Oldsmobile was sucked down by the whirlpool that hit all the manufacturers. Excess, megalomania, frenzy—there is no shortage of epithets to describe the late fifties. The 1958 Oldsmobiles were true battleships, armed to the teeth and covered with metalwork, like knights setting off for the Crusades. Despite this barbaric madness, Oldsmobiles were—partly—spared by the recession of the following years and continued to serve the cause of GM, whereas Chrysler De Sotos, their direct competitors, were abandoned in the early sixties.

This Oldsmobile is teeming with the typical gimmicks of the American cars of the period, such as the molding that runs from the handle to the rear fender, or the two rear lights shaped like ray guns. As for the dashboard, it is an indescribable mass of chrome.

1957 Ford Thunderbird

Phoenix of Dearborn

In 1957, Ford was already celebrating its fiftieth birthday—half a century marked by the fabulous epic of the Model T, by brilliant commercial success and dazzling racing wins. But at Dearborn, engineering had always taken precedence over aesthetics, and in a certain fashion, the score bequeathed by old Henry seemed incomplete: the firm had never placed its badge on the radiator grille of a sports model. Nevertheless, by presenting the Thunderbird in February 1954, Ford had provided masterful proof that could amaze the public as well as respond elegantly to the attacks of European racers and the firm's eternal rival, GM, which had just unveiled the Corvette.

The man who organized the response was Lewis D. Crusoe. Appointed vice-president and general manager of the Ford division, Crusoe belonged to the generation who had been called on by Henry Ford II to dust off and reorganize the ailing enterprise. Crusoe thought that to regild Ford's image, more exciting cars would be needed. A sports car designed by and for Americans seemed the best solution, to

1957 Ford Thunderbird

judge by the enthusiasm aroused by the European roadsters, with Jaguar in the lead. Crusoe entrusted the project to designer George Walker (who was then only a consultant), while Frank Hershey, head of Ford's style department, also threw his team into the venture.

In February 1953, the project was clearly defined. Despite the constraints imposed by Crusoe, who wanted to use as many mass-produced parts as possible, the team piled on the pressure and three months later, presented the new car to management. Under the influence of Hershey, who saw the new Ford as the direct descendent of the Mercer Raceabouts and Stutz Bearcats, the designers produced plans for a car of exemplary purity. Whereas the Corvette seemed stocky and blunt, the Thunderbird was slender and taut. Nothing disturbed the profile, which ran in a single line from the headlight to the taillight. Even the radiator grille and the various ornaments were both sumptuous and sensible, compared with the exuberance that held sway almost everywhere else. Ford had already won its bet. By wanting to create a refined sports car, the firm had given birth to a legend.

Finding a name for the car was not the least of the problems. Many suggestions were put forward—some exotic, some evocative. Eagle, Apache, Tropical, El Tigre, Roadrunner and Savile were rejected one by one. In the end, designer Alden R. Giberson remembered an old Indian legend about the sacred symbol of the divine bird, the Thunderbird. A short time later, Giberson created the emblem of the bird on a turquoise background.

To the attractions of the car's lines, Ford added the charm of the new Y-block, a 292 ci V-8 that produced 193 horsepower with a three-speed manual gearbox and 198 horsepower when coupled to a Fordomatic automatic.

Strong on all counts, the T-bird was put on the market at the end of 1954, and immediately won great success. Ford had struck home: 16,155 cars were sold in 1955, and the unfortunate Corvette, with only 674 buyers, was roundly beaten.

In 1956, the 292 ci engine increased to 202 horsepower. It was then supported by a 312 ci engine, producing 215 horsepower on the version equipped with overdrive and 225 horsepower with automatic transmission. Aesthetically, the car was distinguished by its Continental kit.

The greatest vintage was unquestionably that of 1957. To enlarge the trunk, which once more housed the spare wheel, Ford lengthened the car; at the same time, the diameter of the wheels was reduced from fifteen to fourteen inches. The front was also remodeled, with the fenders curving around the radiator grille. Refined and lowered, the 1957 T-bird was of rare elegance, underlined by two slender and discreet fins, which started at the door handles.

The range of engines was unsurpassed in 1957. The basic V-8 remained the 292 ci, which increased to 212 horsepower, and the 312 ci with its 245 horsepower was mounted in versions equipped with overdrive or an automatic gearbox. As an option, the power could even be increased to 270 and 285 horsepower, or for those who could not content themselves with these modest figures, Ford offered a rare

version (only 208 were made) with 300 horsepower. This high horsepower was obtained with the help of a McCulloch supercharger, which made it possible to go from 0 to 60 mph in less than ten seconds and to maintain a speed of 125 mph on the freeways without losing power.

At the car's highest speed, there was no need to turn up the volume on the radio, since the Volumatic option did so automatically. This equipment, along with the steering wheel with its adjustable height and the electrically controlled windows and seats, revealed Ford's concern to elevate the T-bird above the rank of a mere sports car, pure and simple.

Sales, which had fallen off a little in 1956, put on a new spurt and reached 21,380 in 1957. In the eyes of the financiers, this figure was too modest compared with the 1,670,000 vehicles produced by Ford that year. The T-bird's exclusive character should not have been allowed to prevent the car from being profitable, however, and the managers marked out a new course for it.

Ford's answer to Chevrolet, or sport as seen by Dearborn. Equipped exclusively with a V-8, the Thunderbird, which was launched in 1955, immediately supplanted the Corvette. In 1957, the car sported its first fins. The dials, on their metallic background, add a sporting touch to the dashboard.

1957 Lincoln Premiere

In desperate search of identity

Lincoln once again completely overhauled its range in 1956, and its new line marked a total break with the previous one. This radical change was not the first: for almost ten years, Lincoln had been searching for an identity. First there had been the "globular" period from 1949 to 1951, then a more conformist stage from 1952 to 1955, with fairly conventional cars. Finally, with the new models, Lincoln opted for a tighter, more vigorous design. But such jumps in aesthetic mood, such incoherence of character could not consolidate a brand image. Cadillac, on the other hand, completely understood this, and having solidly established its style, devoted its energy to parading and affirming its image.

In 1956, Lincoln was one of the last manufacturers to adopt the wraparound windshield. The profile of the new models, distinctly more imposing than the previous ones, consisted of a single straight line, finishing at the front and the back with two pronounced beveled edges. The general appearance was inspired by that of the Futura dream car,

1957 Lincoln Premiere

whose headlight visors were repeated. At the rear, a grille with horizontal bars recalled the design of the radiator grille, and the exhausts were hidden inside two chrome-plated nozzles, two pseudo jet engines. The automobile industry was keen on these aeronautical symbols, synonymous with power and supremacy.

For good measure, Lincoln also offered a new engine in 1956. The V-8 with overhead valves, with its 341 ci and 225 horsepower, was replaced by a more vindictive unit of 368 ci, which gallantly produced 285 horsepower. But this engine's power was nothing compared with its colossal torque, a stump-pulling 400 lb-ft at 2800 rpm! By just pressing on the accelerator, you could, without a jolt, move the car's two tons and glide along the Pacific, accompanied only by the muffled sound of the exhausts.

In 1957, power increased to 300 horsepower and the Lincolns rivaled the Cadillacs. But that year was above all marked by the appearance of the first fins. The designers created no details; they simply installed two sharp strips of steel, two slender spurs that elongated and slightly hardened the general appearance. The radiator also underwent the inevitable alterations. The main novelty was the appearance of double headlight inserts, an original arrangement that was to gain a following.

While Cadillac offered eleven different versions in 1957, Lincoln included only seven in its catalog. These were divided into two series: the Capris, which were the basic models, and the Premieres, which were provided with all the equipment necessary to satisfy a demanding clientele— electric windows, seats and top; air conditioning; power-assisted brakes and steering. But this was a time for outdoing your rivals, and since 1956 the Lincolns had been distinguished by two new ideas: safety belts in the front seats, and an original arrangement that enabled you to grease the various elements in the front wheel-axle unit by pressing a button on the dashboard.

Despite all these efforts, Lincoln did not manage to worry Cadillac. Good year or bad, it produced three times fewer cars than its rival—41,123 Lincolns compared with 146,841 Cadillacs in 1957. The prices were, however, close; this Premiere cabriolet cost $5,381, while an equivalent Cadillac cost $5,293.

Lincoln was still looking for a direction, and the 1958 range was once again marked by a complete restyling. This time, the cars were massive and angular, overladen with moldings and ornaments that did not produce the best effect.

Production fell inexorably until 1960. In 1961, however, all such hesitation was swept aside. Thanks to the talents of Elwood Engel, the Lincolns introduced a distinctive style, combining cubism with elegance. The firm finally displayed its real character, and managed to preserve it throughout the sixties.

For ten years, Lincoln searched hard for an identity. In 1956, these cars were given a wraparound windshield and their first fins. Look at the fearsome lights at the end of the fenders of this 1957 Premiere.

1958 Ford Fairlane 500 Skyliner

Taking off the top

A sumptuous red-and-white Ford coupe glides up to the lights. Suddenly, the trunk opens with a mechanical movement and the roof rises slowly before disappearing into the trunk, which smoothly closes again. The driver then puts the lever in the Drive position and pulls away with hissing exhausts, under the stunned gaze of onlookers. This is a Skyliner, a hardtop coupe that, just by pushing a button, can transform into a convertible.

In the mid-fifties, manufacturers were locked in a merciless combat, making great use of fins and unusual gadgets. No holds were barred in the attempt to amaze the public. In this extravagant race, the Ford Motor Company sometimes seemed a little timid and its models often appeared less bold than those of its competitors. But it caused a stir when it unveiled the Skyliner in 1957. The public, although used to the follies of the manufacturers, rushed to admire this metallic monster, not knowing that the car was no more than an accident of strategy, a recovery orchestrated by the marketing department.

1958 Ford
Fairlane 500 Skyliner

Credit for this complicated creation was due the Lincoln division. In July 1953, under the leadership of John R. Hollowell and Ben J. Smith, a study commenced for a retractable hardtop intended for the future Continental Mark II. Management had not hesitated to invest $2.19 million to perfect this roof, and it was completed within eighteen months. Various studies and several successive projects led to the creation of a model that was ⅜ actual size. Needless to say, this model was carefully prepared. Nevertheless, on the day of the presentation to the entire senior management, when the trunk opened, it was catapulted into the arms of the engineers! There was a silence, then everyone burst out laughing. Smith was pale but relieved—no price would be put on his head!

At last, in the middle of 1955, the final prototypes were perfected and the car could be put into production. This was the moment chosen by management to notice that sales of the Continental Mark II would probably not be sufficient to absorb the study's costs. There was no question of abandoning the project, and the model consequently found itself at Ford, where the retractable roof was quickly adapted to the body of the future Fairlane of 1957. By coincidence, this car, which was already well defined, had a trunk that was large enough to contain the hardtop. Ford had narrowly missed an absolute loss of several million dollars!

In total, seven electric motors and more than thirty relays and other electrical contacts were necessary to activate the mechanics. Fortunately, it was easy to use. Beneath its spectacular appearance, however, the Ford concealed some disadvantages. The trunk, already encumbered by the mechanism, was reduced to the capacity of a mere glove compartment when it had swallowed up the hardtop; the spare wheel, placed right at the bottom, was hard to get at; and the trunk opened in the opposite direction to normal and was not easy to load. None of this prevented customers from acclaiming the car, and 20,766 were sold. In any case, 1957 was a good year for Ford, which took first place from Chevrolet.

With great enthusiasm, management therefore decided to bring the car out again in 1958, with a few aesthetic alterations. The front, with its double headlight inserts, and the rear were now inspired by the new Thunderbird.

Ford took this opportunity to alter the Fairlane's specifications. The 272 ci V-8 was replaced by a 292 ci V-8, producing 205 horsepower. As options, two new engines made their

Cars with retractable roofs are rare in the history of the automobile. The Ford Skyliner was produced between 1957 and 1959. This 1958 model sports fins that are modest in comparison to what was being produced by Chrysler or GM, but it redeems itself with its wide molding of yellow metal.

1958 Ford Fairlane 500 Skyliner

appearance. With 332 ci, the first could produce either 240 or 265 horsepower. The second was a 352 ci engine, attaining 300 horsepower. This last engine, which was also provided for the T-birds, gave the Fairlane 500 Skyliner a maximum speed of 125 mph. Ford also offered a new automatic three-speed gearbox, called the Cruise-O-Matic. And, to fill up their last moments of spare time, the engineers perfected an air suspension system, whose simplicity contrasted with that of the system developed by GM. But customers were unimpressed and ignored this option, which was abandoned at the end of the year.

To prove the reliability of all these innovations, Ford sent a Fairlane 500 to all the roads of the world. From London to Calcutta, the car crossed eleven countries without breakdown. As for the hardtop mechanism, it remained unchanged; only the roof, which cracked on 1957 models, was reinforced.

Despite all these improvements, sales fell to 14,713 in 1958. In the end, customers were more traditional than had been thought. They clearly preferred the simplicity of a classic ragtop or a conventional hardtop, which were bought by 35,029 and 80,439 people, respectively. Unless the public's choice had been dictated by ecomomy as the 1958 Skyliner was the first Ford, apart from the T-bird, to exceed $3,000 (it cost $3,163), while a Sunliner ragtop cost only $2,650 and the equivalent coupe only $2,435.

Even with this clear setback, Ford persisted, and in 1959, the Skyliner again appeared in the catalog. It was now included in the Galaxie series, Ford's new top-of-the-line model. The body was unique, yet with its discreet and sometimes flat fins, it remained sensible compared with the grandiose and extraordinary machines of the competition.

But all Ford's efforts were in vain, and at the end of 1959, only 12,915 cars had come off the production line. After an extravagant parenthesis lasting three years, the Skyliner folded back its hardtop for the last time and took its place in the archives, where it slumbers beside the other amazing gizmos of the fifties.

The art of turning a coupe into a convertible, or how to amaze your neighbors in 45 seconds. A simple button on the dashboard activates the 30 or so electric motors, relays and electric contacts which open the trunk, fold back the hardtop, slide it into the trunk and shut it.

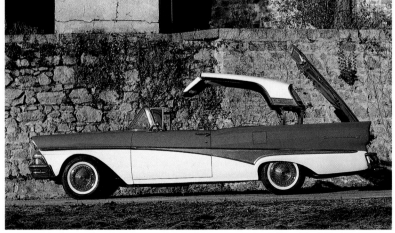

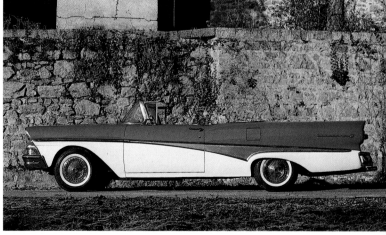

1958 Chrysler New Yorker

Under the sign of equilibrium

In 1958, the French elite abandoned themselves to the joys of the DS Citroen, while the bourgeoisie, who led a comfortable but hard-working existence, enjoyed the more austere pleasures of the Peugeot 403. In the United States, the former drove Cadillacs or Lincolns, while the latter sampled the charms of a Chrysler New Yorker.

Since the late thirties, the New Yorker name had formed a permanent part of the manufacturer's heritage, and in a certain fashion, the New Yorker was the pivot of the range, the link between the popular models and the more luxurious series. In the late forties, this car lived in the shadow of the Town & Country, whose chassis and mechanics it borrowed, without having their finish. Up until 1954, it played a supporting role to the Imperial. From 1955 onward, it was eclipsed by the explosive 300, which monopolized the racetracks.

The New Yorker benefited from all the Chrysler innovations. In 1951, it was given the Hemi V-8, and in 1957 it was equipped with the new front suspension with torsion bars,

1958 Chrysler New Yorker

which gave it above-average roadholding properties. Its style profited from the finest pencil strokes of Virgil Exner, at the peak of his art. And fins made a reasonable appearance in 1956, before rising clearly and flawlessly in the following year.

All this leads up to 1958, with the Chrysler range made up in the following manner. At the bottom of the scale was the Windsor—another legendary series—with its 122 inch wheelbase and a "small" 354 ci V-8 producing 290 horsepower. Next came the Saratoga, which was longer—with a 126 inch wheelbase—offering 310 horsepower with the same engine. Then there was the New Yorker, built on the same chassis as the Saratoga, but equipped with a bigger engine, a 392 ci putting out 345 horsepower. Finally, at the peak, came the 300 D, which defied the competition, containing beneath its generous hood a thoroughbred 380 horsepower engine.

The New Yorker model corresponded perfectly to the needs of a clientele that looked for a certain level of comfort and equipment and that, without attaching undue importance to performance, nevertheless rejected cars that were too easygoing. Chrysler offered six New Yorker models, ranging in price from $4,295 to $5,083; sedans, hardtop coupes and station wagons, as well as a convertible, sold for $4,761 with 666 produced.

The New Yorker's V-8 was coupled to the automatic Torqueflite transmission with three speeds controlled by buttons to the left of the steering column. Still, in 1958, Chrysler introduced the Auto-Pilot as an option on all its models. According to Robert Rodger, chief engineer at Chrysler, this speed regulator constituted an important step toward automatic cruise control driving on the highway. Long tests carried out between Detroit and New York revealed a reduc-

It was only in 1956 that Virgil Exner placed the first fins worthy of the name on Chrysler cars. The 1958 models had sharp blades, but the climax was reached with the 1961 Imperial. With greenish reflections on the dazzling chrome, the cockpit of this New Yorker is like a real aquarium.

1958 Chrysler New Yorker

tion in fatigue (the system, by automatically maintaining the speed displayed, freed the driver's right foot) and a reduction of about fifteen percent in fuel consumption. These two arguments in its favor were all the more powerful since a big development of the interstate road network was planned: in the early sixties, 41,000 miles of fast roads were to link up the large American cities.

After a fashion, Chrysler bore the brunt of the relentless rivalry between Ford and GM, a duel that was to prove fatal for the last independent manufacturers. To ensure their own supremacy and to create a permanent feeling of dissatisfaction in their customers, the two giants from Motor City endlessly renewed their ranges, increased the number of restylings and tried in every possible way at no matter what cost to arouse curiosity. Ford launched its Skyliner with automatic retractable hardtop, while GM touched our deepest fantasies with its fabulous Cadillac Eldorado Brougham.

Chrysler exhausted itself trying to keep up with this unyielding rhythm, and the quality of its models suffered as a result. With the recession that hit the whole economy in 1958 and the strikes that disrupted the manufacturer's production, Chrysler's balance sheet at the end of the year was catastrophic, production falling from 124,675 vehicles to only 63,681 in one year.

The whole group was badly mishandled. Although Plymouth held onto third place, its production fell from 762,231 to 443,799 cars. Dodge division tumbled from 287,608 units to 137,861 and slid from seventh to ninth place, and the De Sotos sank inexorably into oblivion. Finally, Chrysler was suffering, and it looked as if it would make a painful start into the sixties.

With a radiator grille that has three layers of chrome hiding a 345 horsepower V-8 engine, with finely worked hubcaps, with lateral moldings as thick as a lumberjack's arm, with flashy decoration, like this C overlaid with a blazon, the year of 1958 was certainly one of excess. But for Chrysler, which had been buffeted by strikes and criticized for the quality of its cars, it was catastrophic.

1958–60 Edsel Pacer, Corsair and Ranger

Tragicomedy in three acts

The Edsel was the lame duck of American production, the unloved and the outcast. All the specialists have tried to explain the great slap in the face that Ford earned itself with this car, whose name became synonymous with failure. Although the Edsel was no worse than its contemporaries, it seemed that fate, with plenty of help from Ford management, had amused itself in tripping up the brand-new make from its first days of existence.

The farce began in the mid-fifties, when Ford realized that only Mercury was opposing the Buick-Oldsmobile-Pontiac trio of GM. The press soon revealed the existence of a project known by the code name E-car, which was intended to reinforce Ford's position in the middle range. The manufacturer spent a fortune finding a name for this new car, which was unveiled on September 4, 1957. It turned to the poet Marianne Moore and went through more than 10,000 names before finally selecting Edsel, which was the forename of Henry Ford II's father.

1958-60 Edsel Pacer, Corsair and Ranger

Ford had wanted a different car that would not be a shock; it failed. While its competitors sported wide horizontal radiator grilles, the Edsel displayed a vertical one that brought roars of laughter and disgust from all of America. Customers ignored the Edsel; you don't buy a car just to make your neighbors laugh. This was a pity, because the designers, under the aegis of Roy A. Brown, had produced an elegant and taut silhouette, rather pleasing to the eye, with the rear wings designed in a way that foreshadowed, in a more sensible version, the Chevrolet Impalas of the following year. But the fact remained: the average American was allergic to the radiator grille, which made the most obtuse puritans shudder.

Aesthetics alone do not explain the extent of the disaster, however, and many things have been written about the Edsel. It was said that 1958 was the worst year to launch a new make. It was said that the name was wrong. It was said that the Lincoln-Mercury workers, who had been given the task of assembling the Edsel, had not given the required care and attention to the car's manufacture. And, finally and most importantly, it was said that the marketing department had imposed a car that corresponded more to its needs than to the customers' wants. Whatever the truth of the matter, the punishment meted out by the public was severe. Only 63,110 cars were produced in 1958, whereas the most pessimistic estimates had predicted at least 100,000!

Ford had been thinking big and had created a new division, directed by Richard Krafve and detached from Lincoln-Mercury. The Edsel immediately offered a wide range of eighteen models, divided into four series: the Rangers and Pacers, with a 118 inch wheelbase; and the Corsairs and Citations, with a 124 inch wheelbase. Among the sedans, the coupes and the station wagons, the catalog presented two convertibles: a Citation and a Pacer. The first had a 410 ci V-8 producing 345 horsepower; the second was equipped with a brand-new Ford engine, derived from the Y-block, which produced 303 horsepower from 361 ci. Management had deliberately chosen large engines to place the new Edsel unequivocally above the competition.

In 1958, Ford launched the Edsels, a range of models intended to compete with the Buicks, Pontiacs and Oldsmobiles of GM. These cars overflowed with a thousand tricks and had superb equipment, but their radiator grilles made all America howl with laughter and disgust. It was a bitter failure.

1958–60 Edsel Pacer, Corsair and Ranger

This drive to be different, along with the search for a certain form of innovation, explained the presence of some unusual equipment, which completed the Edsel's decline into ridicule. Once again, the car was judged severely; although you could criticize the button controls for the transmission, which were mounted in the hub of the steering wheel, or the presence of a compass, no reproaches could be made about the thermometer for the outside temperature, the drum speedometer and still less the rev counter, an instrument that was quite rare on middle-of-the-range cars of the time.

Shaken by the public's warning shot, Ford beat a retreat the following year. In 1959, the Edsels lost their identity and were no more than disguised Mercurys, although a less elegant version of the rear wings could still be detected. The radiator grille remained vertical but was now flanked by a wide horizontal grille encompassing the double headlight inserts. The range was reduced to ten models, and only two series survived: the Rangers and the Corsairs, built on a single wheelbase of 120 inches.

Ford also reduced the mechanical ambitions of the Edsel in 1959. The 410 ci disappeared completely, and the 361 ci was relegated to the rank of an option. The Rangers and the two Villager station wagons were now provided for by a 292 ci V-8 with 200 horsepower and, on request, could even be driven by a 223 ci six-cylinder engine producing a modest 145 horsepower. The Corsairs were hardly better off: their 332 ci V-8 created 225 horsepower. The only ragtop in the range belonged to this series; it was sold at $3,072, while the Pacer and Citation convertibles of the previous year were worth $3,028 and $3,801, respectively.

To wipe out the affront, Ford was also quick to remove all the unusual gimmicks that had so disturbed people's habits. The Teletouch controls for the transmission were replaced by a classic stick, and the rotary speedometer was put in mothballs.

None of this made any difference; history hounded the car and didn't give it a chance. The debacle worsened, and

In 1959, Ford beat a retreat. The original features of the Edsel were erased and its design was "normalized." The radiator grille preserved its central motif, but was not as prominent as the year before. Unfortunately, all was in vain, and customers continued to ignore these cars.

1958–60 Edsel Pacer, Corsair and Ranger

production fell to 44,891 in 1959, including 1,343 convertibles. But the Edsel was suffering more from Ford's incoherence than from any crippling flaw. America's number two auto maker did not seem to have a group policy. On the one hand, the new Galaxies had settled in the Edsels' yard; on the other, the attention of management, starting with Robert McNamara, was completely taken up by the future Falcon, a compact vehicle on which Ford was basing its hopes for the early sixties.

The proportion of investment granted to the Edsel was reduced to a trickle, and the 1960 models were nothing more than pale Ford derivatives. Only the radiator grille, which had finally lost its vertical position, and the four tapered taillights tried desperately to give an illusion of slight difference. Worse still, it even seemed that at the heart of the Ford Motor Company, the Edsel's fate had already been sealed. How else can you explain the final halt in production only one month after the introduction of the last vintage on October 15, 1959? A total of 2,846 cars were nevertheless produced in this short period.

The range collapsed like a house of cards, but seven versions escaped the wreck: five Ranger models and two Villager station wagons, all equipped with a 292 ci V-8 producing 185 horsepower. The 145 horsepower in-line six engine nevertheless remained available at no extra cost, and a Super-Express V-8, whose 352 ci made 300 horsepower, was a $58 option.

By cutting short the Edsel's career, Ford more or less opened the doors of fame to these cars, which became collector items. This is true of the 1960 ragtop, of which seventy-six were made! Fifty-four have been counted in the United States, but only twenty are in a roadworthy condition, which gives an idea of how rare the model is.

Abandoned by their creators, deserted by millions of Americans (apart from a handful of eccentrics who dared to parade themselves in this car), the Edsels have taken their posthumous revenge. Like the Chrysler Airflow, like the Tucker, they have survived thanks to the enthusiasm of collectors. History owed them this rehabilitation.

Look closely at this car. Edsel only produced 76 convertibles in 1960 and only about 20 are still in circulation! In fact, the production only lasted for the fall of 1959. In total, less than 3,000 cars came out of the factory before Ford put an end to this sad farce.

1959 Cadillac Eldorado Biarritz

Earl's last fling

The United States went through the fifties as if in a golden dream, while Europe peered across the Atlantic with the greedy eyes of a child outside a shop window at Christmas time. Marilyn Monroe, Elvis Presley and others were the ambassadors of the American way of life. In this slightly naive imagery, pride of place was reserved for the great American car. Its provocative exuberance and opulence have always been a flashy symbol of social success in European eyes. In many respects, a 1959 Cadillac would seem to be the caricature of this symbol, as if it had come straight out of a Fred Quimsby cartoon.

To crown thirty-two years devoted to defining the style of GM cars and imposing his aesthetic ideas on customers as well as on other manufacturers, Harley J. Earl got the designers of the Cadillac Studio, led by Charles Jordan, to work on the most flamboyant car the American automobile industry had ever seen. Although the profile was not any more or less tortured than that of the competition, onlookers were nevertheless fascinated by the two sharp steel

1959 Cadillac Eldorado Biarritz

blades mounted on the rear wings. Unlike the Chryslers, whose tailfins rose gradually from the middle of the car, the Cadillacs had a profile that flew out in a single spurt, forming a deadly slash from the raw metal. This was a long way from the timid lines on the Cadillacs of 1948 and their aeronautical inspiration. In ten years, America had changed its heroes. The conquest of space had replaced the exploits of World War II aviation. The Cadillac designers could not ignore this evolution, as is shown by the red lights that shine like four flames from the tailfins of this interstellar vehicle.

One decisive stage in the explosion of style was the Eldorado Brougham. Presented as a show car in 1956 and produced on a small scale in 1957, this car provided a precise definition of Cadillac's aesthetic options for the coming years: a lowered silhouette thanks to a new chassis, double headlight inserts and above all, tapered fins. The 1959 models combined these extras elegantly, while also taking them to the extreme. Afterward, no one would dare to do better—or worse!

Customers reserved a favorable reception for Earl's last fling: after the general slump felt by the American auto industry in 1958, Cadillac increased its sales considerably in 1959 and produced 140,170 cars, compared with 119,863 the year before. However, the golden age of chrome monsters seemed to be under threat. Although the name Ralph Nader was not yet appearing on the front pages of the papers, criticism was already being heard from all sides. People in the press, the public and government commissions all pointed their fingers at the automobile, calling into question its lack of security and the pollution it caused. Even its dimensions no longer met with unanimous approval; the owners of some parking lots started to grant reduced rates to small cars. In defiance of these accusations, the 1959 Cadillacs were creating a magnificent legend.

According to a tradition that was well established with this manufacturer, the range, which included thirteen models in 1960, offered two convertibles: the 62 Series and a more luxurious creation, the Eldorado Biarritz. Unlike in 1958 and 1959, the two cars received the same body and could only be distinguished by the finish: the Eldorado had a good 200 lb. of additional chrome. As if all this was not enough, the Eldorado's rear grille, which dominated the dazzling mass of the fenders, included three superimposed rows of miniature overriders, while the much more peaceful 62 Series had to make do with only one! To satisfy the most unexpected tastes, the customer could choose between eight colors for the interior leather and five colors for the top, combinations allowing the most unusual of cocktails to be composed. Offered at $5,455 each, 11,130 62 Series cabriolets were produced; the Eldorado Biarritz was much rarer, with 1,320 being sold at $7,401 each.

The V-8 that equipped these cars was directly derived from the engine with overhead valves created in 1949. After an increase in cylinder capacity in 1956, it underwent another course of treatment in 1959 and reached 390 ci. This unit produced 325 horsepower on 62 Series models, which could receive as an option, the Eldorado's engine with its 345 horsepower, obtained with the help of three dual carburetors.

The 5,150 lb. of chrome, cast iron and steel thus glided along the freeways at 110 mph. The driver could also sample the soft comfort offered by pneumatic suspension, provided as standard on the Eldorado and as an option on the 62 Series. With the automatic gearshift lever in Drive, all he or she had to do was keep a negligent finger on the power-assisted steering wheel—without thinking of the future and the slow decline of the fins.

Before leaving the scene, Harley J. Earl achieved a great feat and left us the most famous fins in the history of the automobile. The Eldorado could be distinguished from the more "common" Cadillacs by several pounds of additional chrome. The dashboard remained diabolically beautiful. Note the Autronic Eye in the center; this automatically lowers the beams when you meet another vehicle.

1960–61 Chrysler 300 F and 300 G

Brawny charm

The hierarchy established at Detroit had always classed Chrysler in third place, behind the giants of Ford and GM, and never gave this outsider the opportunity to disturb the duel for first place. The Highland Park firm nevertheless managed to punctuate its history with some sublime creations. First was the Airflow in the thirties; next came the Town & Country series after World War II; and then came the 300 Letter Series, an elegant creature appearing in 1955.

More fantastic than a Corvette or a T-bird, the 300 did not, however, have that thoroughbred style which contributed to the creation of the Chevrolet and Ford legends. For reasons of economy, Chrysler had decided otherwise, and this formidable machine sported the body of a quiet New Yorker. When driven, however, it was scarcely possible to confuse the two cars. The 300 was a real dragon, capable of confronting a Jaguar XK 150 or a Mercedes 300 SL.

The spiritual father of these two superb animals—the 300 F and 300 G—was Robert Rodger, Chrysler's chief engineer, an affable and discreet man who was as brilliant as Charles

1960-61 Chrysler 300 F and 300 G

F. Kettering, his counterpart at GM. In the late forties, Rodger made a significant contribution to the development of the fabulous Hemi Firepower V-8. Presented in 1951, this 331 ci engine produced only 180 horsepower, but had incredible potential exploited by Briggs Cunningham, whose C5R car came in third at Le Mans in 1953, behind two C-type Jaguars. Rodger also envisaged taking full advantage of the possibilities offered by this engine. He conceived of a car that was bare but powerful.

Rodger was tenacious and defended his project till the end; thus, on January 17, 1955, Chrysler presented the first 300. The Firepower underwent some modifications for this car: the camshaft was reinforced, the valves were mechanically controlled to withstand high engine speeds and the whole system was force-fed by two enormous dual carburetors. This vigorous arrangement increased the horsepower to 300, fifty more than in a New Yorker and the highest rating on the market. For $4,110, you could buy a beast that could go from 0 to 60 mph in nine seconds and cruised at nearly 130 mph. This animal was all the more wild because the power-assisted steering and brakes, the electric windows and seats, the clock and even the heating were available only as options!

Through the years, the 300 became less crude, but in 1960 the 300 F was still formidable. Nevertheless, things had changed in five years. The cars had followed the style of the other Chryslers, and since 1957 they had sported neat and elegant fins. In 1960 and 1961, lashing sabers started at the foot of the windshield and rose in a single swoop up to the taillights. As for the radiator grille, it was a large black mouth flanked by double headlight inserts. Although the style was not completely sober, the cars nevertheless escaped the aesthetic frenzy that had hit the Imperials.

The 300s' reputation as monsters still rested on their engine. Since 1959, the Firepower V-8 had given way to a more conventional engine that kept the overhead valves but abandoned the hemispherical cylinder heads. The new unit was lighter than the Firepower V-8, although just as ferocious with a capacity of 413 ci. In 1960, it could create either 375 or 400 horsepower, according to choice. This machine got its strength from the Ram system, a resonator that compressed the incoming air and crammed the cylinders. All there remained to do was adjust the length of the manifolds in favor of either torque or power.

Chrysler 300 . . . the very name makes you tremble. Behind the gaping mouth slumbers a formidable V-8 which produces 375 or 400 horsepower, according to choice. The 1960 300 F sports sharp fins and a wheel impression on the trunk. The seats pivot and invite you to take the wheel of this formidable mount.

1960-61 Chrysler 300 F and 300 G

The new system was ingenious and produced plenty of power. Although the Torqueflite automatic transmission was standard, the 400 horsepower versions could also have a manual four-speed gearbox, increasing performance still further. Strangely enough, Chrysler chose a French gearbox made by Pont-a-Mousson. Only seven cars of the 1,212 produced were equipped with this gearbox, and those cars were sold to racing drivers—one of whom, Gregg Ziegler, was timed at more than 145 mph on the Daytona track!

The fittings were no longer as rudimentary as at the beginning, and the 300s now combined power with refinement. Among other things, they had pivoting front seats; the central support was extended and separated the rear seats, making the 300 a strict four-seater; and the driver faced a console that would make the most imaginative science fiction scriptwriter blush with shame!

In 1961, the 300 G succeeded the 300 F. The mechanics remained unchanged, although the Pont-a-Mousson gearbox was abandoned. Despite the inevitable aesthetic alterations, the style retained all its charm. From the front, the 300 G could be recognized by its double headlight inserts mounted in a V; at the rear, the boomerang-shaped red lights had left the tips of the fins.

With a total of 1,616 cars, including 337 ragtops, production was slightly improved in 1961. Prices had not gone up one cent: the hardtop remained at $5,411 and the convertible at $5,841.

In 1962, the power of the Chrysler 300 H reached its peak at 380 and 405 horsepower, but the fins were clearly defined. Prices fell by about $350, which did not prevent sales from slipping.

In 1963, it was the power's turn to collapse. It fell to 360 and 390 horsepower on the 300 J and L in 1963 and 1964, then to only 360 horsepower on the 300 L of 1965, the last in this prestigious lineage.

After the abandonment of the De Sotos, Chrysler thus gave up one of its finest legends. In the course of the sixties, however, the American automobile was to be the victim of a witch hunt, and Chrysler would not be alone in counting the cost.

In 1961, the 300 G succeeded the 300 F. The designers had made alterations to the headlights and the taillights, but the car was still just as diabolical. In any case, how can you doubt their intentions when you are confronted by this science fiction console?

1961-62 Imperial Crown

They had to take the risk

If a prize had to be given to the most bizarre car, the Imperial Crown of 1961 would probably win it. This was an inexplicable and indescribable car, a tortured sculpture to be observed without comment. Eyes looked in vain for peaceful angle, rational minds could not comprehend it and people found it hard to decide whether they were contemplating diabolical beauty or bewitching ugliness. Nothing could justify such extravagance, except the mad arrogance of a designer at the twilight of his career.

The man in question was Virgil Exner, head of Chrysler design since 1950. Until 1956, his inspiration came from the gentle elegance of the Italian school. Then in 1957, there was a sudden change of course and Exner became even bolder than Harley J. Earl. Chryslers began to acquire fins that were as brutal as the stabilizers on fighter planes—the Forward Look came into being.

1961–62 Imperial Crown

With 37,593 cars, the Imperial's results for 1957 were encouraging, but this success was completely overturned the following year. To cap it all, Exner persisted, and the tortured design of the Imperials continued to be overloaded.

In the early sixties, Imperials were looked on as monsters on the verge of extinction. The 1960 model was an important step on the road to bad taste; the 1961 was the pinnacle of extravagance. At the front, the four headlights were completely separated from the body and were sheltered under a fold of sheet metal made by the wings; at the rear, the two sharp spurs ended in two taillights suspended in midair! On the trunk, the shape of a false spare wheel completed the neo-classical appearance. Only the sides, which were emphasized by a wide chrome molding, retained an uncluttered appearance.

The interior's beauty was just as acidic, and it was preferable to examine it through dark glasses. First was the four-cornered steering wheel, which didn't turn smoothly. Next were the two banks of push buttons arranged in a V on each side of the steering wheel, with the automatic transmission controls on the left and the subsidiary controls (windshield wipers, headlights and so on), which you could reach without letting go of the steering wheel, on the right. Then the seat, which pivoted toward the outside, allowing drivers to get in without effort. Finally the dashboard, an indescribable mixture of chromeplated metal and bright red plastic, more like the control panel of a cosmic vehicle in a cartoon than the dashboard of an automobile.

The convertible was built on a standard and unique 129 inch wheelbase, and under its vast hood it had a Chrysler V-8, also fitted to the New Yorkers, which produced a brisk 350 horsepower from its 413 ci. This was coupled to the Torqueflite automatic gearbox, a three-speed transmission system that had appeared in 1956.

A total of 429 convertibles finally left the Warren Avenue factory in 1961, a derisory figure if you compare it with the 1,450 total for the Eldorado Biarritzes, which were considerably more expensive at $6,477 compared with the Imperial's $5,774. This gap was indicative of Cadillac's supremacy; that year, it produced about ten times more cars than did Imperial: 138,379 compared with 12,258.

Faced with this obvious failure, Lynn Townsend, Chrysler's new manager, decided to give up. The Warren Avenue plant was sold, and Imperial returned to the Jefferson Avenue factory, to the buildings vacated by the departure of De Soto. Virgil Exner was thanked and replaced by Elwood Engel, recruited from Lincoln, where he had just designed the brand-new Continental.

The design of the Imperials gradually settled down, but the cars kept their neo-classical headlights until 1963. The following year, the firm unveiled its new range, which renounced all exuberance and became an exercise of pure geometry. For the first time since 1957, production exceeded 20,000. Imperial never succeeded in worrying Cadillac, nor even Lincoln, and in 1975, the name disappeared without a trace—until 1980, when Chrysler retrieved it from oblivion to designate a luxury coupe. For fifty years, the third-biggest American manufacturer had been trying to get in the way of its two inaccessible rivals. For fifty years, it had been plagued by its top-of-the-line complex, a stubborn old demon that never stopped tormenting it.

With its taillights suspended in midair and its neo-Classical head-lamps, completely detached in style from the bodywork, the Imperial casts a last challenge at those who would later make auto-mobile design banal. The interior is ablaze in sharp red reflections, spar-kling chrome and a wraparound dashboard. Is this a car or a spaceship?

1962 Cadillac Eldorado Biarritz

Transformation

At the start of the sixties, there was a radical change in the aesthetics of the automobile. This transformation was particularly marked in the United States, where, in less time than it takes to polish the chrome on a 1959 Cadillac, the American car gave up its resounding lines, its downstrokes and upstrokes, in favor of a geometric style, finally admitting that the straight line was the shortest way to join the front fender to its counterpart at the rear. The baroque period now belonged to the past, and design studios were preparing to enter the era of cubism. At GM, Harley J. Earl had just retired and handed over his place to Bill Mitchell.

The automobile's transformation was part of the logical course of history, but this transfer of power at GM was probably also one of its causes. Earl had always displayed his jovial and exuberant character in opulent and extravagant bodies, while the tendencies of Mitchell, who was more peremptory and incisive, were translated into a barer style that was both tight and vigorous.

Mitchell marked his arrival at the end of 1959 with the Chevrolet Corvair. With its smooth, lucid surfaces, contrasting with the remains of the baroque monuments from the

1962 Cadillac Eldorado Biarritz

decade that was ending, the new car presented the main themes of the aesthetic revival in the United States.

Cadillac also underwent a process of purification, but in a less brutal fashion. The first victims were the fins. Having reached their pinnacle in 1959, they lost their superb arrogance the following year. However, the designers must have had misgivings about removing these glorious appendages, because what they removed from the top, they added at the bottom. The Cadillacs may have had less ambitious spurs, but they did not have fewer spurs; the cars now sported four: two above the wings and two below. All things considered, the overall effect had not gained in serenity.

The real break with the fifties was probably marked by the 1961 abandonment of the wraparound windshield, the aesthetic gimmick that had been introduced in 1953 by the Eldorado and happily sported by American cars for nearly ten years. The year 1962 was marked by only a few minor alterations: a new radiator grille, rectangular turn indicators instead of circular ones and a new arrangement for the taillights—these were the only features of the vintage. Cadillac had adopted a biennial rate of renewal, and the great aesthetic changes did not come until 1963.

Technically, developments of the make did not disturb public order. The main innovation was the 1957 adoption of a new X-shaped chassis, which was more rigid and which allowed the center of gravity and the general lines of the cars to be lowered; Cadillac used this until 1964. The engineers also perfected a pneumatic suspension system, reserved for the Eldorado Brougham in 1957 and then offered as an option on other models until 1960—but its lack of reliability caused it to disappear.

The Kettering V-8 came to the end of its days with the Eldorado Biarritz. In 1956, its cylinder capacity went from 331 to 356 ci, with an increase in bore, and in 1959 it went to 390 ci, thanks this time to a longer stroke. In 1962, this unit produced 325 horsepower on all models, including the Eldorado, which since 1961 had no longer enjoyed any

advantage of power. In 1963, the veteran was retired. Cadillac had perfected a new V-8, also with 390 ci but lighter and quieter, more compact and rigid and having new development potential. Cadillacs urgently needed this new, more vigorous engine; for some time, they had been unable to claim any sort of engineering supremacy. Within GM, the Buick Electra, the Oldsmobile Starfire and the Pontiac Bonneville were of equal and sometimes even greater prowess. Even the Chevrolets could have, as an option, a 409 ci V-8 that produced 409 horsepower!

Fortunately, Cadillac remained without equal as regards comfort, luxury and refinement. Earl, among others, had worked in this direction throughout the fifties, the 1953 Eldorado and the 1957 Brougham having pushed this ostentatious luxury well beyond the limits of the rational. The 1962 models, particularly the Eldorado Biarritz, retained his heritage. The voluptuous carpet, fine leather, hood, seats, windows, including the electrically controlled ventilating windows, air conditioning and cruise control, Autronic Eye, and four cigarette lighters were all signs of this desire to be different.

A total of 160,840 cars left the factory in 1962, and Cadillac kept its tenth position in the hit parade of manufacturers, a place it had won in 1958 at the height of the economic recession. Throughout the sixties, production never stopped increasing, and it reached 200,000 in 1967. Cadillac seemed to be sheltered from all turmoil. It had managed to set itself up as a symbol, one that still exercises fascination today.

The fins were less arrogant than in 1959, but they were as sharp as razor blades. And the Cadillac now had four of them, two on top of the wings and two others below. The style nevertheless settled down a little, but the luxury remained just as stunning.

1962 Ford Thunderbird

Thunder rumbles
for a third time

The question is on everyone's lips: did the T-bird die in 1958? Yes, if you side with the purists; certainly not, in the eyes of history and the sales figures recorded by the models that succeeded the Little Bird. The least that can be said is that Robert McNamara, who replaced Lewis D. Crusoe as Ford president at the end of 1954, was not an automobile fanatic. His passion was more for figures, especially when they took the form of a positive balance sheet.

As soon as he took office, McNamara erased the two-seater T-bird from his worries. Were the customers asking for four-seaters? Well, the customers' wishes would be granted. Thus, in 1958, the T-bird was succeeded by—the T-bird! Yet, although the name remained, the new Ford had little to do with the previous models. The elegant, thorough-bred bird had given way to a large, gaping whale, whose aesthetic qualities were tortured and vulgar. Nevertheless, two or three interesting ideas were introduced, such as the unit body and the suspension with four helical springs

1962 Ford Thunderbird

(which was soon abandoned). The engine made considerable progress, but the notion of sports car became a distant memory. On the other had, the new T-bird opened up a new avenue, into which the competition would surge: this was the avenue of personal luxury cars, which nevertheless had to remain mass-produced and, if possible, widely distributed.

Although the original spirit of the car was no longer there, the direction taken by the T-bird pleased its customers, and sales rose to nearly 200,000, including 24,255 convertibles, in the years 1958-60.

In 1961, after the now-traditional three-year cycle, the third generation of T-birds entered the scene with, once again, another radical change in aesthetics. This time, the silhouette regained its serenity and the car presented only smooth, neat surfaces. In profile, the shape was reminiscent of a fuselage and—a sign of the times—the windshield lost its panoramic curves. The beltline molding, which was emphasized by a chrome-plated trim that included the door handle, rose from the front tip of the car and went in a gentle slope toward the rear, ending in two enormous round lights that glowed red like the nozzles of two jet engines. The inspired designer who produced this stroke of genius was Bill Boyer. Boyer had been in charge of design in the Thunderbird department since 1955, and his project prevailed over that of Elwood Engel, who was attached to George Walker's studio and whose work acted as a basis for the development of the 1961 Lincoln Continental.

Among other innovations, the 1961 T-bird introduced an electric windshield wiper motor and an entirely transistorized car radio. But most amazing was the steering wheel, which could be swung to the right to make it easier to slide into the driver's seat. This option, requested by three quarters of all customers, would be delivered as standard in the following year.

In 1962, the Sport Roadster version appeared. Lee Iacocca had replaced McNamara at the helm of Ford in 1959; although just as pragmatic as his predecessor, Iacocca was not hostile to sports models that enhanced the image of the make. To appease those who were still mourning the first T-bird, he decided to develop a more exclusive model. There was no question of devoting huge sums of money to the affair, but despite its tiny budget, the operation was successful. The back seats were encased by a fiberglass tonneau cover forming a back behind the headrests. The car also sported superb Kelsey-Hayes wheels, and the cockpit contained a sissy bar for nervous passengers.

This model was one of the finest T-birds that ever existed, but it was provided with the same mechanicals as the rest of the range. The four versions in the catalog—coupe, coupe landau with vinyl roof, ragtop and Sport Roadster convertible—were all equipped with the 390 ci V-8, which produced 300 horsepower and was adopted by the whole range in 1961. As an option, this unit could produce 340 horsepower with the help of three Holley dual carburetors.

Despite its uncluttered aesthetic qualities, the Sport Roadster attracted only 1,427 customers in 1962, a figure that fell to 455 in 1963. The extra cost of this model compared with the cost of a conventional convertible amounted to $651, but customers must have disliked drafty cars because the coupes won the most votes, selling 69,554 of a total 78,011 T-birds in 1962.

In 1964, Ford launched the fourth generation of the T-bird. The design remained pleasant, but the car had lost some of its shine and the divine bird was no longer so magical. It was now being deserted in favor of another fabulous animal, a galloping pony that, ten years after the first T-bird, marked the beginning of a new legend.

In 1961, the T-birds gave up the wraparound windshield and acquired sharp lines. Although it is only a standard model, this convertible is equipped with a fiberglass tonneau cover which covers the rear seats and is normally reserved for the Sports Roadster versions. You can get in effortlessly thanks to the large bowl-shaped steering wheel which moves to the right.

1963 Chevrolet Corvair

Bad reputation

Whether out of a sense of fun or by economic necessity, small European cars such as the Volkswagen Beetle achieved fame in the United States during the fifties. This story would have remained just an anecdote if the sales recorded by these little pests had not given the American manufacturers the bitter impression that they had foolishly abandoned a share of their own cake. They were obliged to react. Thus appeared the Studebaker Lark and Rambler Custom, followed late in 1959 by the Ford Falcon, Plymouth Valiant and Chevrolet Corvair.

The Corvair could have aligned itself with the technical similarity of its competitors, but GM decided otherwise, adopting unusual solutions. A unit body and, above all, flat-six engine were the principle features of the new little Chevy. This car also sported sharp, uncluttered lines that contrasted sharply with the flamboyancy of the last monsters of the Harley J. Earl period. The shining chrome had disappeared, the voluptuous curves had been abandoned, the missile-launcher fins had been removed. Under the

1963 Chevrolet Corvair

same price, the Corvair offered considerably less brilliance, and it could not struggle against this tidal wave.

At GM, a final maneuver was attempted. The 1965 Corvair was completely redesigned. The taut silhouette of the car was softened by sober and elegant curves, similar to those of the Buick Riviera, and the radiator grille was made more aggressive. The new models lacked neither charm, distinction nor attraction, but their bad reputation stuck and customers did not line up for them. Tired of these repeated failures, GM decided to cut the venture short and planned to halt production at the end of 1966.

The Corvair could have coasted along to the end of its career without causing a stir—but fate had decided to have a go. On November 25, 1965, America was presented with a book by Ralph Nader, *Unsafe At Any Speed.* Quoting numerous statistics and making use of thousands of police reports, Nader accused Detroit of producing mobile coffins, of having put power before safety, of having deceived the public by bringing out badly designed models and of having built up profits without investing in research. First among the accused was the Chevrolet Corvair, which was called into question because of its teething problems, but whose enormous steps forward were ignored.

At GM, Nader's indictment was a thunderbolt. In the offices of Detroit, they seethed with anger, they smashed telephones and they sent out armies of detectives to investigate the private life of this advocate of misfortune. Nader was irreproachable. He was an honest citizen without stain or vice. The affair went before the courts, the authorities got involved. It was a repeat of David and Goliath, but the show was not to the taste of the managers in Motor City and they had to admit defeat. For its punishment, the American automobile industry was crushed by blind legislation, which was intended to improve the safety and design of vehicles but which, cloaked in good intentions, was to kill off all that the automobile had in the way of emotion and passion.

Stopping the production of the Corvair during this storm would have amounted to an implicit acknowledgment of Nader's accusations. GM therefore decided to prolong the career of this lame duck; despite all the maligning it had received, the Corvair found another 103,743 buyers in 1966!

From the commercial point of view, the car was dead, but Chevrolet continued to carry it at arm's length for some time, keeping it in the catalog only out of defiance and to satisfy a few devoted enthusiasts. Since 1967, GM has had a much more effective weapon in the Camaro, which replied point by point to the Mustang. Finally in 1969, the managers decided to put an end to the career of the Corvair; during its last year of existence, it appealed to 6,000 more customers, the last handful of fans.

influence of Bill Mitchell, the GM designers had produced a car that seemed to have come straight from an Italian studio.

The Corvair was available for about $2,000, but customers ignored it in favor of much more conventional cars, such as the Chevrolet Biscayne, which offered a certain standing and were closer to their aspirations. To cap it all, serious rumors called into question the car's oversteering characteristics and its uncertain stability. The little Chevy had obviously stumbled during its entrance into the ballroom.

GM quickly became aware of its mistakes, and a few months later, in May 1960, it launched a new and more pleasing version, the Monza coupe. This was still not a revolution, but with its less lugubrious presentation and the option of a 95 horsepower engine, it attracted a younger clientele. The Corvair seemed to have found its direction.

In 1962, the catalog finally included a convertible. But the great novelty was the appearance of the Spyder versions, coupe and convertible, whose engines, fed by turbochargers, leapt in one go up to 150 horsepower. Performance underwent the same improvement: speed now reached 111 mph instead of 87 mph, and 0-60 could be achieved in 10.7 seconds instead of the previous 20.2 seconds. The list of novelties was completed with a four-speed gearbox and above all, much more effective suspension, wiping out the original flaws. Being better armed, the 1962 Corvair enjoyed a temporary success, and production, which had been about 250,000 in 1960, reached 300,000.

This was still a long way from the scores achieved by the Falcon, which was about as sophisticated as a skateboard but sold some 400,000 vehicles per year. Nevertheless, the nonconformist character of the Corvair had revealed the existence of a market oriented toward a young, relatively well-off, slightly snobbish, although not completely fringe clientele, who were enthusiastic about the 150 horsepower Monza Spyder versions. Ford had understood the message about "horses from a thoroughbred line"; here, in short, were the specifications for the future Mustang, which was to inaugurate the era of the pony car and flood all America. For the

With a flat-six engine mounted at the rear, with a particularly bare line and basic equipment, the Chevrolet Corvair is a unique case in the history of the American automobile. It was only in 1962 that the catalog was blessed with a ragtop and with models of higher performance. These were equipped—for the first time in mass production— with a turbocharger.

1964 Studebaker Lark Daytona

South Bend,
a dead-end street

At Studebaker in South Bend, Indiana, the accounts had been in the red for a long time. From year to year, however, those in charge, obliged to work with existing models, had tried to redress the balance of the doyen of the American automobile. In 1958, Harold Churchill, the new president of the automobile division, thought Studebaker's salvation would be brought about by a popular, economic model of reduced dimensions, like the small European cars whose success was irritating the managers in Detroit. Unfortunately, Churchill did not have the means of the three big companies, and once again, it was necessary to use leftovers; this is what he explained to Gene Harding, chief engineer, and Duncan McRae, head of design. The future car would therefore keep existing elements, notably the central structure, which dated from 1953! The chassis was shortened, however, and new suspension systems were studied. In the end, the delicate and thankless task of designing the future model fell to Virgil Exner, Jr., and Bill Bonner.

1964 Studebaker
Lark Daytona

Seven months after Exner and Bonner began, when the Studebaker Lark was unveiled, the public was presented with a squat and thickset car. Fortunately, the new small car preserved a family likeness with the Hawk, whose trapezoid radiator grille was flanked by two small horizontal air inlets it inherited. Despite its lack of aesthetic qualities, the new Lark immediately won great success, which confirmed beyond all hope Churchill's forecasts and allowed Studebaker, for the first time since 1953, to make a profit, amounting to $29 million!

In 1960, Ford, GM and Chrysler sounded the charge on the compact car market and launched their Falcons, Corvairs and Valiants. Lark sales collapsed: 109,781 cars left the factories, compared with 160,826 in 1959.

Churchill continued to believe in the virtues of his car and planned an ambitious program for 1962, but Clarence Francis, president of the group, did not share the same aims. Francis preferred to devote the sums initially set aside for the development of the Lark to the purchase of prosperous businesses. The two men argued and on September 2, 1960, Churchill left the Studebaker Corporation. Francis now had a free hand to follow his policy of diversification and allow the Studebaker group to make substantial profits in the years to come, while the automobile division was collapsing.

Churchill was replaced by Sherwood Egbert, who launched Studebaker into the era of the Avanti. In parallel with this exceptional car, Egbert contacted designer Brooks Stevens and asked him to touch up the other models for 1962. The Lark's style was modernized and refined. The car was made longer, and the radiator grille was now flanked by double headlight inserts. The Daytona finish also appeared, and was used to support the Cruiser models at the top of the line.

Even with all these efforts, Studebaker seemed to be condemned. In November 1963, Egbert, depressed and ill, handed over to Byers Burlingame, whose only ambition seemed to be to hasten the end. One month later, Burlingame announced the transfer of production to the Hamilton factory in Canada, and on December 9, 1963, the last Studebaker left the South Bend factory.

A sad end for the Studebakers, whose production, which had been transferred to Canada in late 1963, would be halted once and for all in 1966. However, the last Larks were not lacking in charm, with their angular lines designed by Brooks Stevens. Regarding the mechanics, this Daytona convertible could take eight different engines, with power ranging from 182 to 335 horsepower!

1964 Studebaker Lark Daytona

Despite this exodus, Stevens accomplished some remarkable work and presented a 1964 vintage that was still more elegant. The Lark range was transformed. This time the pencil lines were decisive and the curves that had survived were finally replaced by a tauter, more vigorous design, which gave the illusion of increasing the car's length. The new radiator grille, which was lower and wider and encompassed the double headlightts, harmonized perfectly with the angular rear, mounted with two slender horizontal lights. For the sake of balance, the two ribs that ran around the front and rear wheelhousings were symmetrical.

Although it was in its last days of existence, the 1964 Lark range was blessed with four finishes—the Challenger, Commander, Daytona and Cruiser—able to take an in-line six engine of 169.5 ci and 112 horsepower or a V-8 of 259 ci and 180 horsepower. A large catalog of engine options meant the customer could choose among a vast range of V-8s, from the 259 ci increased to 195 horsepower to the 304.5 ci, which produced 335 horsepower.

This Daytona cabriolet enjoyed the standard 259 ci V-8, a small engine that allowed the car to reach speeds of up to 106 mph. This was certainly not enough to frighten the average American, but the Studebakers were mainly appreciated for their qualities on the road. The automatic gearbox, called Flightomatic, had three speeds, and the car could also be equipped with a manual gearbox with three or four speeds. Front disc brakes were optional in the United States but standard for export. Inside, you could detect the hand of Stevens, who was attached to the details of equipment, as revealed by the vanity mirror in the glove compartment.

Although they were made in Canada, the last Studebakers perpetuated the heritage of this make, which has always managed to distinguish itself from its competitors. In 1965, the cars underwent further alterations, but it was too late, and production stopped definitively on March 4, 1966. This end was all the more lamentable because the Studebaker Corporation, which included a multitude of firms in different sectors, was in the process of expanding. But financiers do not suffer from uncertainties, and they signed the death warrant for the automobile division, that doyen founded in 1852 by the Studebaker brothers, who settled at South Bend on the road West, to make carts.

This ragtop is one of the last representatives of a famous dynasty which had been established at South Bend, Indiana, since 1852. The Studebaker brothers had chosen this spot on the road to the West to make and repair wagons for the pioneers.

1965 Ford Mustang

Crazy horse

In 1960, the United States was getting younger. John F. Kennedy was elected to the White House, and the percentage of twenty to twenty-five year olds, born in the postwar baby boom, would double in the coming years.

At Ford, Lee Iacocca surrounded himself with a young team who were resolved to freshen up the brand image. Market research had shown that the late-fifties fashion for austere and economic models was waning and customers were once again demanding more exciting cars. At the same time, Ford continued to receive large quantities of mail regretting the absence of the first T-birds, suggesting that this car was ahead of its time. Iacocca and his team therefore decided to give America a made-to-measure automobile that was attractive and dynamic, but also inexpensive, so as to reach the greatest number of customers. The idea of the Mustang was born.

The designers immediately settled down to their drawing boards to trace its contours; the success of the future model depended to a large extent on their pencils. By the early summer of 1962, no project had been decided on, however,

1965 Ford Mustang

and as the launch was planned for the New York international fair in April 1964, Iacocca started to get impatient. To speed things up, he organized a contest between the teams of designers, deadline August 19. Seven models were finally presented, but just one of them corresponded to the wishes of management—the one by the Dave Ash, Joe Oros partnership. These two men had designed a car whose long hood exuded an air of elegance and aggressiveness and whose rear, which was short and stocky, gave an impression of restrained power. Because of its feline appearance, the project was called the Cougar. Now everything could go ahead, since most of the drivetrain was to be borrowed from the Falcon.

Outlined, defined and positioned in the market, the new car was looking for an identity. As with the T-bird ten years. earlier, there were plenty of suggestions, but the choice for a name finally fell on Torino, a name that evoked the perfumed exoticism of Italy. But, a few weeks before the presentation, an event put Dearborn in turmoil: Henry Ford II had just gotten to know a young Italian woman. The name of the car had to be changed immediately, or the gutter press would be unleashed. Someone was given the urgent task of examining the bestiary that was so dear to Ford. He produced six names: Bronco, Puma, Cheetah, Colt, Cougar and Mustang. The last met with unanimous approval, especially since this name had already been used for a prototype, a choice that had been inspired by the P-51 fighter plane from World War II.

The Cougar's silhouette had won Iacocca's enthusiasm; the Mustang, which was delivered to dealers on April 17, 1964, was to unleash the crowd's passions. On that day, America was set alight and everyone hurried to admire the new Ford, which aroused great covetousness. A frenzy took hold of all four corners of the United States. In Texas, a man spent the night in the car exhibition hall so as not to be dispossessed of his property, which he had beaten off fourteen other customers to acquire at the auction the day before! In Seattle, the driver of a concrete mixer who was fascinated by the Mustang pulverized the garage window, and many dealers could not contain the enthusiasm of the inquisitive. The press latched onto the story, and the Mustang appeared simultaneously on the front pages of *Time* and *Newsweek,* an unprecedented occurence.

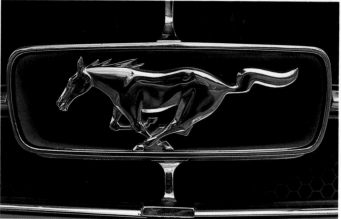

With its squat rear suggesting power and its long, slightly aggressive hood, the lines of the Mustang, designed by Dave Ash and Joe Oros, aroused the enthusiasm of America. The wild horse unleashed at a gallop has become legendary. However, the car was very nearly called Cougar or Torino.

1965 Ford Mustang

Ford had envisaged 75,000 first-year sales. The numbers were quickly revised to 200,000 cars. In the end, 418,812 Mustangs were sold in one year! The Falcon's record had been beaten.

It must be said that the car offered its attractions at a particularly advantageous price. For example, a softtop cost only $2,368 in 1965, putting it in direct competition with the Chevrolet Corvair and Dodge Dart, which were already old and much less exciting. What was more, customers could personalize their cars as they wished by selecting from an impressive list of options allowing them to improve the equipment, change the presentation and choose the transmission. They could even transform the Mustang into a real sports car, thanks to a large choice of suspension systems and disc brakes. These options also enabled the "poor" six-cylinder engine, with its 170 ci and 101 horsepower, to be replaced by a 260 ci V-8 of 164 horsepower.

In the fall of 1964, Ford made some adjustments. The in-line six was replaced by a more generous 200 ci engine with 120 horsepower, and a new V-8 appeared as an option: the famous 289 ci engine that could produce 220, 225 or 271 horsepower, depending on the wishes of the customer; in the more powerful versions, the engine would soon grace the Cobra and GT40.

Born from the pragmatic and intuitive mind of Iacocca, the Mustang quickly crossed the Atlantic. With the abundant help of racing and the movies, the myth became established in Europe, to the point that it has now become inseparable from the legend of the sixties.

This convertible is probably one of the most beautiful on the roads of Europe. A V and three figures on the front fender show that it is equipped with the 298 ci V-8, the famous 4.7 liter Ford engine, which would serve as a basis for the Cobra and GT40 engines. It is also provided with the Rally Pac option, which supplements the instrumentation with a rev counter and a clock.

1965 Chevrolet Corvette Sting Ray

Superb beast

The Sting Ray should no doubt be classed among the ten most fabulous cars that have ever existed. In the first place, there is the car's unique style, a refined feline design that makes an immediate impact on you; it is probably Bill Mitchell's masterpiece. Then, there is the desperate search for ever more power, orchestrated by Zora Arkus-Duntov, who, in 1967 concocted the most monstrous Corvette of all time, an extremely rare version equipped with the L88 engine producing 560 horsepower.

Like all the first Corvettes, the Sting Ray was created in secret. Recall that the Automobile Manufacturers Association forbade its members to take part in racing in 1957; consequently, the Corvette SS, a prototype intended to oppose the greatest makes in races such as the Sebring 12 Hour Race or Le Mans, was killed off at birth. But Mitchell decided to buy back this experimental car, and on its base he created a new racer, which he ran privately in 1959 and 1960. The results obtained were modest, but the car attracted attention mainly because of the beauty of its form. For

1965 Chevrolet Corvette Sting Ray

observers, the equation was simple: this special Corvette foreshadowed the revival.

The 1961 vintage Corvettes provided a glimpse of the future. Without being entirely redesigned, the cars were given the famous ducktail, with its characteristic distinct ridge and its four little round lights, identical to those of the future Sting Ray.

In parallel with Mitchell's project, three other cars were developed to replace the Corvette, but in the end none of them was judged satisfactory and they were abandoned.

Finally, in 1963 Chevrolet officially presented the new Sting Ray. The great revelation was the appearance beside the traditional two-seater roadster of a fastback coupe, distinguished by its split rear window. Mitchell had decided on this stylistic effect, intended to emphasize the whole of the car's backbone so as to accentuate its stocky appearance and its aggressiveness. All his collaborators had opposed this original feature, and the press heaped criticisms on it. In the end, Mitchell retreated and the split window was gone in 1964. The coupe also sported disappearing double headlights; this was the first time since the 1942 De Sotos that an American model had been given retractable headlights. Among the main reproaches aimed at the coupe was the absence of a trunk that was accessible from the back; you had to load the luggage over the seat. The roadster was free from this criticism, but its general lines lacked the originality of the coupe, although it still radiated elegance and harmony.

Not only the design was new. The Sting Rays had also been given a brand-new chassis, which was more rigid than the old, and a new suspension system with four independent wheels, which pushed back further the car's limitations and allowed the adoption of a more formidable engine.

There were four Sting Rays in 1963, and their engines remained identical, for the moment, to those of 1962, the year of the great changes when the 283 ci engine was changed to 327 ci by a simultaneous increase in bore and in stroke. With carburetors, these cars reached 250, 300 and 340 horsepower while the fuel injection versions produced 360 horsepower.

The years that followed produced some fireworks. In 1964, the table of specifications announced 250, 300, 365 and 375 horsepower.

In 1965, a new step was taken with the appearance of a new optional unit, a 396 ci engine belonging to the Mark IV Turbo-Jet family producing 431 horsepower. Thanks to this engine, the Sting Ray could reach speeds of up to 140 mph and could do the quarter-mile trip in fourteen seconds.

The indefatigable engineers had already made this new engine bigger by 1966. Its cylinder capacity increased to 427 ci, producing 395 and 430 horsepower. It supplanted the old 327 ci engine, which now existed in only two versions of 300 and 350 horsepower.

As a final touch, in 1967 the Turbo-Jet boasted horsepower of 405 and 441, without forgetting the phenomenal 560 horsepower version. Remarkable for their power, these engines also distinguished themselves with their monstrous torque, which could reach as much as 462 lb-ft delivered

unrestrainedly at 3600 rpm and above. This animal power struck anyone who took the Sting Ray's wheel. The many tests were unanimous: depending on axle ratio, performances differed by a few hundredths, but by and large, a Corvette in top condition equipped with a 429 ci engine could do 0-60 mph in five seconds, could run the quarter-mile in twelve seconds and could cruise at around 137 mph. The Sting Ray had only one real rival, the Shelby Cobra, which was just as monstrous but much more Spartan.

By deciding to produce Mitchell and Arkus-Duntov's Sting Ray, Chevrolet thus made the right decision, and although not astronomical, the production figures nevertheless made regular progress, going from 21,513 in 1963 to 22,229 in 1964, 23,562 in 1965 and 27,720 in 1966, before settling at 22,940 cars in 1967. The Corvette's qualities explained a large part of its success, but the prices probably also had something to do with it. Oscillating between $4,000 and $4,400 depending on the version and the year, they were below those of the T-bird, which was admittedly aimed at a clientele more attracted by luxury and comfort than by strong sensations.

In any case, Ford was not yet claiming the label of sports car (although that would soon change with the Shelby Mustang). On the other hand, this label stuck only too well to the Sting Ray. Trying to get rid of it would be a difficult task; even the following generations of Corvettes would not manage to do so. Today, the Sting Ray is still considered the most fabulous American sports car of all time.

The Chevrolet Corvette Sting Ray is Bill Mitchell's masterpiece. Its heavy-set lines suggest power—generously provided by an army of V-8s, the most monstrous of which puts out 560 horsepower! Everyone who has sat at the wheel of this car, opposite the two arches of the dashboard, has been impressed by the strength of this dragster.

1966 Chevrolet Chevelle SS

Hot oil and burned rubber

What do we remember of Chevrolet in the sixties? The Sting Ray, of course; the Camaro, too; and, for quite different reasons, the Corvair. But this leaves out a whole generation of models: the Chevelle Super Sports. At first sight, these Chevys have nothing that could arouse interest and blend in with the rest of their fellows. The Chevelle's appearance is not unpleasant; the problem is that it lacks flavor. The eye runs from the radiator grille to the taillights without the attention being held by anything. Even if you look at it ten times, it does no good; your memory will slide on these contours as on the soapy bottom of a bath.

In the fifties, at least, beautiful American cars knew how to get themselves admired. The curves and contours only became blurred so as to better regain their momentum. The shapes were nothing but swoops and arabesques, and the manufacturers devoted their energies to modeling those exuberant sculptures. But the Chevelle came into being in 1964, in a period when American design was rediscovering the virtues of geometry. Why, in these conditions, did this car slip among those sumptuous ragtops? Simply because it

1966 Chevrolet Chevelle SS

represented the muscle car, a generation of dynamite models launched at a good price by all the manufacturers.

To concoct these bombshells, auto makers used the simplest of formulas: an economic and average sedan with the largest possible V-8 installed in it. The result was explosive. These cars burned as much rubber as fuel at each traffic light, glided along enthusiastically, cruised at more than 125 mph, braked with much less elation—in short, they appealed to the deepest knowledge of the art of driving. The more skillful found in them an incontestable source of wild pleasure; the less-well-informed exposed themselves to some memorable close shaves. Each manufacturer offered its own recipe. Ford developed the Fairlane GT and then the Torino GT, while Chrysler defended its colors with the Dodge Charger Hemi and the Plymouth Road Runner. In a certain fashion, GM was the most active, simultaneously offering its customers the Pontiac GTO, the Oldsmobile 442 and the Buick Gran Sport.

In 1964, when the Chevelle was launched, the problem was mainly to fill the gap between the compact Chevy II and the large Impala. The problem was also to offer an intermediary model to erase the failure of the Corvair. Having burned its fingers with this unhappy experience, Chevrolet was careful to avoid any technical audacity and even re-adopted the good old solution of a separate chassis, whose simplicity was enough to make you shudder (it was so rudimentary that on the first models, it started to break in some places!). All the rest was in keeping, so that the rear suspen-

sion, which was entrusted to helical springs and not to mere plates, seemed revolutionary.

From the start, the Chevelle range offered three series— 300, Malibu and Malibu SS—giving a total of twenty-two different versions, equipped with a multitude of engines. At the bottom of the scale were two peaceful six-cylinder engines, one with a capacity of 194 ci producing 120 horsepower, the other with a capacity of 230 ci giving 140 horsepower. Next came the whole V-8 spectrum. The standard Chevelles were equipped with a 283 ci engine producing 195 horsepower, or 220 horsepower as an option. The most interesting of all was the famous 327 ci engine, available only as an option on the Malibu SS, which could produce 250 or 300 horsepower, according to choice. In 1965, Chevrolet took another step forward and provided the SS with the brand-new 396 ci Turbo-Jet V-8, which was capable of producing 325, 375 and even 425 horsepower. The result was truly terrifying.

These cars were real dragsters whose favorite pastime was to burn up the tarmac. All versions could do 0-60 mph in less than seven seconds and the quarter-mile dash in less than fifteen seconds. Unfortunately, they were at a complete loss when required to show a little agility. Of the three models, the most usable was the 375 horsepower one. It combined the attraction of the small 325 horsepower engine with the strength of the 425 horsepower engine, thanks to a special camshaft, large valves and an enormous Holley quad carburetor. In addition, it was the best off as far as torque was

concerned. The 418 lb-ft produced at 3600 rpm and over, propelled you toward the next light before your adversaries had even got into first.

In 1966, Chevrolet seemed to want to repent. The 396 was still to be found under the Chevelle SS's hood, but while its standard version still had 325 horsepower, the option had to make do with 360 horsepower. Although torque was still just as vigorous, performance marked a slight retreat: it took about eight seconds to go from 0 to 60 mph and 15.5 seconds to cover the quarter-mile with the maximum speed around 125 mph. These results could still vary depending on whether the car was equipped with a manual gearbox with three or four speeds, or the automatic Powerglide with liquid cooling. The customer could also choose among five different axle ratios, varying from 3.31:1 to 4.88:1, the last three having limited slip.

This was also the year of the first restyling. Like the Corvairs, the Chevelle's design was influenced by the style of the Buick Riviera, from which the gentle forms, the elegant movement of the rear fenders, the aggressive radiator grille and the hollow rear were borrowed. All the models were in the same boat, and the Malibu SS could now be distinguished from the basic versions only by a few sets of initials, the 396 on the radiator grille, crossed flags on the front wings, flashy ornaments and artificial air scoops on the hood. The cockpit contained all the ingredients typical of the period. Behind the bowl-shaped steering wheel and its chrome plated spokes, the massive dashboard contained a rectangular speedometer that was hard to read. The other information was entrusted to simple indicators, and the rev counter (which was delivered only as an option, as was the clock) was mounted in the central console, which was not particularly practical.

One thing was certain: Chevrolet was not trying to attract customers with pleasing equipment. The aim was to provide sensation at a low price. At $2,776 for the coupe and $2,984 for the convertible (plus $105.35 for the 360 horsepower engine), 72,300 customers sampled the terrible delights of the 1966 Malibu SS. Even today, it is not uncommon to hear the low throb of a well-supplied V-8 and to see one of these (slightly faded) beasts go past, leaving a waft of hot oil behind it.

The Chevelle belongs to the muscle car category, the category of cars that look peaceful but which are equipped with fearsome V-8s and which burn up as much rubber as gasoline each time they pull away. As for this ragtop, it contains the famous 396 ci 375 horsepower engine originally designed for the Corvette! Look at the rectilinear style of the dashboard, typical of the sixties.

169

1969 Ford Fairlane 500

Race to win

Ford wanted to blow the dust off its name, revive its energy
and give itself a more dynamic reputation. The year was
1962, and Lee Iacocca was already dreaming up the Mustang. In the big office in Dearborn, management had a
brilliant idea: rather than spend its energy creating a new
image for itself, Ford would treat itself to a glorious, prestigious and magical one—the senior managers simply decided
to buy Ferrari!

The Americans arrived at Maranello acting as if they were
going to a supermarket: "Help yourself and pay when you
leave." Enzo got angry and sent everyone back across the
Atlantic. Negotiations were broken off before they had even
started, and Ford was obliged to get its hands dirty.

If there was one person who rejoiced in this setback, it was
Carroll Shelby, who was consequently given funds to
develop the Daytona coupes. In 1964, these cars ran off with
the world title under the very noses of the Ferrari 250 GTOs!

1969 Ford Fairlane 500

But Ford wanted a win at the legendary Le Mans twenty-four hour race.

In 1964 and 1965, the American manufacturer got into its stride, and in 1966, Bruce McLaren and Chris Amon took their seven-liter GT40 Mk II to victory. In 1967, it was the turn of A. J. Foyt and Dan Gurney, at the wheel of a GT40 Mk IV, again with a seven-liter engine. Officially, Ford then decided to retire, but its name remained closely linked to the GT40s entered by Briton John Wyer, who won at Le Mans in 1968 and 1969.

Ford had won its bet. It was now intimately linked to racing, especially since the V-8 developed in Great Britain by Frank Costin and Keith Duckworth, the famous Ford Cosworth, was just beginning a glorious career in Formula One.

Despite all this success, Ford had not neglected its regular customers: those who, at the beginning of the century, had made Ford's fame and fortune by remaining faithful to the famous Tin Lizzie for nearly twenty years; those who, in the early sixties, had voted for the Falcon, a compact car that was nevertheless austere and lacking in charm.

The Falcon was still in the catalog in 1969, but to satisfy a clientele that was looking for a little more attraction and comfort, Ford offered the Fairlane range. Since 1955, this intermediary sedan had been the joy of the middle classes and a formidable rival of the Pontiacs and Plymouths. In the late sixties, it did not escape the rule that was typical of American production: the customer could make up his or her own automobile from a vast range of options that, in particular, offered a choice of engines varying from 155 to 335 horsepower. The standard versions were equipped with a 250 ci in-line six, providing the least power. For greater enjoyment, Ford offered four different V-8s. The first had a capacity of 302 ci and produced 220 horsepower. The second reached a capacity of 351 ci and provided a choice between 250 and 290 horsepower. The third boasted 320 horsepower from a cylinder capacity of 390 ci. The fourth was a 428 ci engine, producing 335 horsepower, which was also found under the hood of the Mustang Mach I. As if this was not enough, the Fairlanes were supported by the Torino series, which were charged with defending the Ford colors in the muscle car arena. To effectively counter the Chevelle SS and Dodge Charger, the Cobra version of these cars was immediately given the fire-breathing 428 engine.

Even with its elegant and sober contours, the only convertible in the Fairlane range, selling for $2,651, met with little success, and Ford delivered only 2,264 of them in 1969. The manufacturer also offered a convertible in the Torino GT series; another superb and much more representative one built on the base of the Galaxie 500; and a third, still more imposing one in the XL range. At Ford, as elsewhere, the word convertible was synonymous with luxury and splendor, and the convertibles that were most successful were also the most expensive and most sumptuous. Thus Ford sold 6,910 Galaxie 500 convertibles for $3,159 and 7,402 XLs for $3,297.

In 1970, the Fairlane ragtop disappeared from the catalog. The other convertibles were also condemned: faced with a lack of interest from customers and increasingly severe legislation, Ford would call a definitive halt to the production of convertibles in 1973. Number two of Detroit had other priorities; it now concentrated its efforts on the small sedans. After the Maverick in 1970, it launched the Pinto in 1972, for which it had perfected an in-line four engine. Ford had not produced such a small engine for thirty-nine years.

Ford won its fourth consecutive victory at Le Mans but still did not forget its traditional clientele—the clientele that had given it success in its medium cars, like this Fairlane 500. Although the seventies were close, there was still plenty of chrome, and the dashboard, with its round dials, was curiously suggestive of the late forties.

1976 Cadillac Eldorado

The sun also sets

People gradually gathered around the production line. The night shift had remained behind after the relief team arrived. Some retired workers had even returned to watch. The assembly line was nevertheless following its normal rhythm, a slow and inexorable pace. Just as on every other day, chassis advanced, engines were mounted, and bodies, ornaments and accessories were fitted, with everything bathed in the characteristically thick and heady odor of grease, glue and fresh paint. But this was April 21, 1976. At exactly twelve minutes past 10 o'clock, Ed Kennard, director since 1974, took the wheel of the car that came to the end of the production line. Applause was heard. Cadillac had just produced its last convertible. It was white, and the manufacturer decided to keep it as the symbol of a bygone tradition.

Cadillac announced its decision to halt the production of convertibles at the end of 1975. The customers immediately went wild. They rushed to the dealers, who were overcome with orders. Buyers suddenly realized that this was their last chance to acquire one of the most prestigious cars in the

1976 Cadillac Eldorado

world. In Nebraska, one businessman ordered six, and in Kansas, another ordered seven. In Detroit, management was submerged by insistent letters, written by fanatics, pleading their enthusiasm, their loyalty and their attachment to the make so as to win the honor of acquiring one of the last Eldorado ragtops.

To face up to this tidal wave, senior management decided, in January 1976, to create a Last Convertible committee, supervised by William J. Knight, director of public relations. Knight decided to commemorate the event by decorating the last 200 cars, which were all identical and painted an immaculate white, with a plaque announcing that these were the last convertibles of the make—and of the United States, since Chrysler and Ford had given up this type of model in 1971 and 1973, respectively. To satisfy the great demand, Cadillac produced 14,000 cars—a record amount; since its reintroduction in 1971, the Eldorado convertible had never reached 10,000 cars per year. The official price was $11,049, but on the secondhand market the rates for this historic model quickly rose.

The Eldorado was given the largest Cadillac engine, but this 500 ci V-8, strangled by the antipollution laws, could produce only 190 horsepower. For some years the manufacturer had been reducing the compression ratio of its engines so they could use lead-free gasoline. Thus, from 235 horsepower in 1971, the power fell to 210 in 1974 and 190 horsepower in 1975. In this period Cadillac also decided to announce the net power of its engines rather than the gross value. The only transmission system available was the GM three-speed automatic Turbo Hydra-matic gearbox. The Eldorado had front-wheel drive, which Cadillac had adopted for this range of models in 1967, while the other series preserved the classic arrangement.

Despite the recession and the increasingly apparent craze for small foreign sedans, these cars still managed to retain their impressive dimensions. Since 1971, the Eldorado's wheelbase had reached 126.3 inches and the monumental appearance of the car, which was eighteen feet eight inches long, was still accentuated by the vehicle's massive and angular design. Nevertheless, in reply to changes in the market, Cadillac had, in the previous year, presented the small Seville—at least it looked compact in comparison with its sibling models.

In 1976, Cadillac was the last American manufacturer to offer its customers a convertible. With its imposing dimensions, its distinctive angular design and its abundant chrome, this Eldorado is the worthy heir of the model that was launched in 1953.

1976 Cadillac Eldorado

It has often been said that American convertibles were killed off by the weight of legislation, which imposed strict standards, especially in cases of vehicles rolling over. But this severity does not explain everything. Some responsibility lies with the customers, whose tastes tended to point them toward coupes with vinyl roofs and air conditioning. Faced with such slack demand, the manufacturers gradually withdrew, and the production of convertibles in the United States went through a long period of eclipse during which a handful of faithful enthusiasts had to make do with the T-bar roof.

Fortunately, the start of the eighties was marked by a renaissance of the real convertible, and for this we should be thankful. Even if these true convertible coupes remain on the fringe, even if they attract only a few dedicated followers, they are expressions of both passion and elegance—two key words that, when brought together, have given rise to some prestigious cars.

Despite the constraints and restrictions that weighed down the American automobile, this Cadillac has lost none of its haughtiness and arrogance. Luxury is present everywhere, as can be seen from the wide seats covered in supple leather, while symbols of elitism abound, like these lights engraved with the insignia.

178

179

1987 Chevrolet Corvette

Heiress

Some legends have a hard life. For example, the Corvette has managed to remain the symbol of the American sports car, but the seventies, which were in any case severe years for the economy, gave a particularly rough ride to this car of myth. The oil crisis, recession, antipollution and safety laws—leading to the disappearance of convertibles in the United States—constantly changed the automobile industry. For the Corvette, this chaotic period ended in a permanent reduction in power and performance. In 1975, the 350 ci compact V-8, which had appeared in 1969, produced a meager 165 horsepower (or 205 horsepower as an option), and the large 427 ci engine had been swept away in the storm. To cap it all, in the course of this decade, the Corvette lost its two spiritual fathers. Zora Arkus-Duntov retired in 1974—which did not prevent him from continuing to devote most of his time to the Corvette—and Bill Mitchell followed him three years later.

The men who took over control of the Corvette's destiny—David R. McLellan as technical manager and Jerry Palmer in charge of Studio Three, the design section—

1987 Chevrolet Corvette

proved to be equal to the mission they had been assigned: designing the eighth generation of Corvettes. Before the arrival of these two men, the existing team had already planned the successor for the beginning of the eighties. The project, which was called Aerovette and was ready to go into production, was conspicuous because of its central engine. In the early seventies Chevrolet had even developed versions equipped with two- and four-rotor Wankel engines, providing a total of 420 horsepower. But the Aerovette never saw the light of day. In the first place, the Corvette was selling well and those in charge did not consider it urgent to find a replacement for it. In the second place, in 1975 and 1977 Porsche produced the 924 and 928, whose structure contradicted Chevrolet's options. Finally, and above all, with the departure of Arkus-Duntov and Mitchell, the project had lost its two most ardent supporters, and McLellan was a fervent supporter of the traditional outline.

In 1978, Palmer and McLellan's teams set to work. The secret of their success had much to do with their collaboration, and not one bolt on the car was studied without consultation. What is more, the two men had pinpointed the exact problem: they had to eradicate the faults without destroying the character of the car. The future Corvette had to be aerodynamic, more spacious, still more efficient, but it should still be possible to recognize it at first glance.

It was the end of 1983 at the Riverside circuit in California when the press was introduced to the new Corvette. The car had not rejected its aesthetic origins, and although it was considerably smaller than previous versions, it was just as impressive from the sides. The designers' great achievement was to have masterfully modernized the contours without breaking with the past. The overall effect was both tauter and more slender. The joint between the wheelhousings and the wings was hardly noticeable, and the sides no longer curved inward so much, which allowed the width of the cockpit to be considerably increased.

The interior style, the work of Pat Furey's team, was absolutely in keeping with the whole. The design was sober and modern, but some features were judged too futuristic. This was true of the instrumentation, which was digital and displayed the various information numerically in a feast of colors. The mechanics were under permanent surveillance from the onboard computer. The seats, covered in supple leather, could optionally have six electrically adjustable positions, and three inflatable cushions in the back made it possible to adjust lumbar support. In addition to this, the angle and height of the steering wheel could be adjusted so that any driver could find an ideal position.

The greatest technical change was the abandonment of the classic chassis in favor of a central beam onto which the frame of the car was soldered before it was covered by the body panels, which were still made of fiberglass. The seventies had had at least one beneficial effect: to reduce fuel consumption, the engineers had searched for every possible

The fortunes of the Corvette were now in the hands of Jerry Palmer (design) and David R. McLellan (technology)—two men who proved equal to their task. The last generation of Corvettes, launched in 1983, was no less successful than the previous ones, even if some of the decisions taken were definitely modern, like the digital instrumentation.

1987 Chevrolet Corvette

way of reducing the weight. Thus in 1981, the helical springs had been replaced by a simple transverse plate made of fiberglass, an original feature still found today, both at the front end and at the rear. For the same reason, aluminum was used everywhere: Chevrolet chose it for the driveshaft and supports, suspension arms, central chassis beam and even the brake calipers. As for the air filter, it was made of magnesium alloy!

All those who had deplored the decline in performance were reassured in 1983. The new Corvette still inspires respect. When you turn the ignition key, the muffled rumbling of the V-8 hits you in the stomach. Of course, the big 427 ci engine has disappeared, but the 350 has retained some fine leftovers from it. Thanks to its double electronic injection and double Crossfire ignition, it produces 240 horsepower on a 1987 model and above all, has a vigorous torque of 344 lb-ft at 3200 rpm, making the windows shake when you restart the machine. The Corvette can thus go up to 140 mph and goes from 0 to 60 mph in seven seconds. The more reckless can treat themselves to the Callaway coupe at any Chevrolet dealer, a version that, thanks to the twin turbos, cruises at 177 mph!

The transmission is special as well. The manual four-speed gearbox is doubled by an overdrive that acts on the last three gears, so as to reduce engine speed and consequently, consumption. The driver thus has seven gears at his or her disposal, but when pure performance is desired, he or she can bypass this accessory by flicking a switch on the central console.

After a ten-year absence, the convertible staged a comeback in 1986. It is technically identical to the coupe, but thanks to it, the Corvette has linked up with its history once more. As on all the first models, the manually controlled top disappears into a trunk behind the seats, unveiling a profile as sharp as a blade. Enthusiasts have not waited in vain. This ragtop does not betray the past. It remains the most absolute expression of the sport as seen from America.

In 1987, Chevrolet delivered 10,625 of these convertibles from a total of 30,632 Corvettes. This figure rewards Chevrolet's determination and proves that, sometimes, emotion can win over reason.

Dropped from the catalog in 1976, the Corvette ragtop made a reappearance in 1986. As in all the early models of 1953, the top was hidden under a rigid cover, but the cockpit was no longer so Spartan. For example, the leather seats offer six different positions!

Specifications

Chrysler Town & Country, 1948
Engine　　　　　Standard: 8 cylinders in-line with
　　　　　　　　　　　　　side valves
　　　　　　　　　　　　　323.5 ci
　　　　　　　　　　　　　135 hp at 3,200 rpm
　　　　　　　　　　　　　270 lb-ft at 1,600 rpm
Transmission　　Standard: Semi-automatic gear-
　　　　　　　　　　　　　box with 2 speeds
Dimensions　　　Length: 216.8 in; width: 78 in;
　　　　　　　　　　　　　wheelbase: 127.5 in
Price　　　　　　　$3,395
Number produced　3,309

Chevrolet Fleetmaster, 1948
Engine　　　　　Standard: 6 cylinders in-line with
　　　　　　　　　　　　　side valves
　　　　　　　　　　　　　216.5 ci
　　　　　　　　　　　　　90 hp at 3,300 rpm
　　　　　　　　　　　　　173 lb-ft at 2,000 rpm
Transmission　　Standard: manual 3 speed gear-
　　　　　　　　　　　　　box
Dimensions　　　Length: 197.8 in; width: 73 in;
　　　　　　　　　　　　　wheelbase: 116 in
Price　　　　　　　$1,750
Number produced　20,471

Packard Custom Eight, 1948
Engine　　　　　Standard: 8 cylinders in-line with
　　　　　　　　　　　　　side valves
　　　　　　　　　　　　　356 ci
　　　　　　　　　　　　　165 hp at 3,600 rpm
　　　　　　　　　　　　　280 lb-ft at 2,000 rpm
Transmission　　Standard: Manual 3 speed gear-
　　　　　　　　　　　　　box
　　　　　　　　　　　　　Electrically controlled
　　　　　　　　　　　　　clutch
Dimensions　　　Length: 213 in; width: 77 in;
　　　　　　　　　　　　　wheelbase: 127 in
Price　　　　　　　$4,295
Number produced　1,105

DeSoto Custom, 1949
Engine　　　　　Standard: 6 cylinders in-line with
　　　　　　　　　　　　　side valves
　　　　　　　　　　　　　236.6 ci
　　　　　　　　　　　　　112 hp at 3,600 rpm
　　　　　　　　　　　　　194 lb-ft at 1,600 rpm
Transmission　　Standard: 3 speed manual gear-
　　　　　　　　　　　　　box
　　　　　　　　　　Option:　Fluid-Drive hydraulic
　　　　　　　　　　　　　coupler
Dimensions　　　Length: 207 in; width: 73 in;
　　　　　　　　　　　　　wheelbase: 125.5 in
Price　　　　　　　$2,578
Number produced　3,385

Cadillac 62 Series, 1949
Engine　　　　　Standard: V-8 with overhead
　　　　　　　　　　　　　valves
　　　　　　　　　　　　　331 ci
　　　　　　　　　　　　　160 hp at 3,800 rpm
　　　　　　　　　　　　　310 lb-ft at 1,800 rpm
Transmission　　Standard: Automatic GM
　　　　　　　　　　　　　Hydramatic

　　　　　　　　　　　　　gearbox with 4
　　　　　　　　　　　　　speeds
Dimensions　　　Length: 215.9 in; width: 78.9 in;
　　　　　　　　　　　　　wheelbase: 126 in
Price　　　　　　　$3,442
Number produced　8,000

Buick Super Eight, 1950
Engine　　　　　Standard: 8 cylinders in-line
　　　　　　　　　　　　　with overhead
　　　　　　　　　　　　　valves
　　　　　　　　　　　　　263.3 ci
　　　　　　　　　　　　　124 hp at 3,600 rpm
　　　　　　　　　　　　　225 lb-ft at 2,000 rpm
Transmission　　Standard: 3 speed manual
　　　　　　　　　　　　　gearbox
　　　　　　　　　　Option:　2 speed automatic
　　　　　　　　　　　　　Buick Dynaflow
　　　　　　　　　　　　　gearbox
Dimensions　　　Length: 204 in; width: 80 in;
　　　　　　　　　　　　　wheelbase: 121.5 in
Price　　　　　　　$2,478
Number produced　12,259

Hudson Commodore Eight, 1950
Engine　　　　　Standard: 8 cylinders in-line
　　　　　　　　　　　　　with side valves
　　　　　　　　　　　　　254 ci
　　　　　　　　　　　　　128 hp at 4,200 rpm
　　　　　　　　　　　　　197 lb-ft at 1,800 rpm
Transmission　　Standard: 3 speed manual
　　　　　　　　　　　　　gearbox
　　　　　　　　　　Option:　Automatic Drive-
　　　　　　　　　　　　　Master clutch
Dimensions　　　Length: 207.5 in; width: 75.6 in;
　　　　　　　　　　　　　wheelbase: 124 in
Price　　　　　　　$2,893
Number produced　425

Chevrolet Styleline, 1951
Engine　　　　　Standard: 6 cylinders in-line
　　　　　　　　　　　　　with overhead
　　　　　　　　　　　　　valves
　　　　　　　　　　　　　With manual
　　　　　　　　　　　　　gearbox: 216.5 ci
　　　　　　　　　　　　　92 hp at 3,400 rpm
　　　　　　　　　　　　　175 lb-ft at 1,500
　　　　　　　　　　　　　rpm
　　　　　　　　　　　　　With automatic
　　　　　　　　　　　　　Powerglide
　　　　　　　　　　　　　gearbox:
　　　　　　　　　　　　　235 ci
　　　　　　　　　　　　　105 hp at 3,600
　　　　　　　　　　　　　rpm
　　　　　　　　　　　　　192 lb-ft at 1,600
　　　　　　　　　　　　　rpm
Transmission　　Standard: 3 speed manual
　　　　　　　　　　　　　gearbox
　　　　　　　　　　Option:　2 speed automatic
　　　　　　　　　　　　　Powerglide
　　　　　　　　　　　　　gearbox
Dimensions　　　Length: 198 in; width: 74 in;
　　　　　　　　　　　　　wheelbase: 115 in
Price　　　　　　　$2,030
Number produced　20,172

Studebaker Champion, 1951

Engine	Standard: 6 cylinders in-line with side valves 169.6 ci 85 hp at 4,000 rpm 137 lb-ft at 2,400 rpm
Transmission	Standard: 3 speed manual gearbox
	Option: 3 speed automatic Studebaker/Borg-Warner gearbox
Dimensions	Length: 197.5 in; width: 70 in; wheelbase: 115 in
Price	$2,157
Number produced	Unknown

Packard Caribbean, 1953

Engine	Standard: 8 cylinders in-line with side valves 327 ci 180 hp at 4,000 rpm 299 lb-ft at 2,000 rpm
Transmission	Standard: Automatic 2 speed Packard Ultramatic gearbox
Dimensions	Length: 213 in; width: 77.9 in; wheelbase: 122 in
Price	$5,210
Number produced	750

Cadillac Eldorado, 1953

Engine	Standard: V-8 with overhead valves 331 ci 210 hp at 4,150 rpm 328 lb-ft at 2,700 rpm
Transmission	Standard: 4 speed automatic GM Hydra-matic gearbox
Dimensions	Length: 215.8 in; width: 80.1 in; wheelbase; 126 in
Price	$7,750
Number produced	532

Chevrolet Corvette, 1954

Engine	Standard: 6 cylinders in-line with overhead valves 235.5 ci 152 hp at 4,200 rpm 222 lb-ft at 2,400 rpm
Transmission	Standard: 2 speed automatic Powerglide gearbox
Dimensions	Length: 167 in; width: 72 in; wheelbase: 103 in
Price	$3,523
Number produced	3,640

Cadillac 62 Series, 1955

Engine	Standard: V-8 with overhead valves 331 ci 253 hp at 4,400 rpm 328 lb-ft at 2,700 rpm
Transmission	Standard: 4 speed automatic GM Hydra-matic gearbox
Dimensions	Length: 223.4 in; width: 80 in; wheelbase: 129 in

Price	$4,488
Number Produced	8,150

Packard Caribbean, 1956

Engine	Standard: V-8 with overhead valves 374 ci 310 hp at 4,600 rpm 404 lb-ft at 2,800 rpm
Transmission	Standard: 2 speed automatic Packard Twin Ultramatic gearbox
Dimensions	Length: 218.5 in; width: 78 in; wheelbase: 127 in
Price	$5,995
Number produced	276

Buick Roadmaster, 1956

Engine	Standard: V-8 with overhead valves 322 ci 255 hp at 4,400 rpm 340 lb-ft at 3,200 rpm
Transmission	Standard: Automatic Buick Dynaflow with double reactor
Dimensions	Length: 213.6 in; width: 80 in; wheelbase: 127 in
Price	$3,704
Number produced	4,354

Chevrolet Bel Air, 1956

Engine	Standard: 6 cylinders in-line with overhead valves 235.5 ci 140 hp at 4,200 rpm 222 lb-ft at 3,200 rpm
	Option: V-8 with overhead valves 265 ci 162, 170 or 205 hp
Transmission	Standard: 3 speed manual gearbox
	Option: 2 speed automatic Powerglide gearbox
Dimensions	Length: 197.5 in; width: 73.7 in; wheelbase: 115 in
Price	$2,344
Number produced	41,268

Ford Thunderbird, 1957

Engine	Standard: With manual gearbox: V-8 with overhead valves 292 ci 212 hp at 4,500 rpm 299 lb-ft at 2,700 rpm With overdrive and automatic gearbox: V-8 with overhead valves 312 ci 245 hp at 4,500 rpm

Ford Thunderbird, 1957

Engine
                    329 lb-ft at 3,200 rpm
Option: 270, 285 or 300 hp (with McCulloch compressor for 312 ci engine)

Transmission Standard: 3-speed manual gearbox
Option: manual gearbox with 3 speeds plus overdrive; 3 speed automatic Fordomatic gearbox

Dimensions Length: 185 in; width: 70 in; wheelbase: 102 in

Price $3,408

Number produced 21,380

Lincoln Premiere, 1957

Engine Standard: V-8 with overhead valves
368 ci
300 hp at 4,800 rpm
399 lb-ft at 2,800 rpm

Transmission Standard: 3 speed automatic Turbo-Drive gearbox

Dimensions Length: 224 .6 in; width: 80.3 in; wheelbase: 126 in

Price $5,381

Number produced 3,676

Oldsmobile Super 88, 1957

Engine Standard: Rocket V-8 with overhead valves
371 ci
277 hp at 4,400 rpm
399 lb-ft at 2,800 rpm
Option: Rocket J2 300 hp

Transmission Standard: 3 speed manual gearbox
Option: 4 speed automatic GM Hydra-matic gearbox

Dimensions Length: 208 in; width: 76.5 in; wheelbase: 122 in

Price $3,447

Number produced 7,128

Chrysler New Yorker, 1958

Engine Standard: V-8 with overhead valves
392 ci
345 hp at 4,600 rpm
449 lb-ft at 2,800 rpm

Transmission Standard: 3 speed automatic Torque-Flite gearbox

Dimensions Length: 220 in; width: 79.5 in; wheelbase: 126 in

Price $4,761

Number produced 666

Ford Fairlane 500 Skyliner, 1958

Engine Standard: V-8 with overhead valves
292 ci
208 hp at 4,500 rpm
295 lb-ft at 2,400 rpm
Options: V-8 with overhead valves
332 ci
265 hp at 4,600 rpm
339 lb-ft at 2,400 rpm
V-8 with overhead valves
352 ci
300 hp at 4,600 rpm
393 lb-ft at 2,800 rpm

Transmission Standard: manual gearbox with 3 speeds plus overdrive
Option: automatic Cruise-O-Matic gearbox with 3 speeds

Dimensions Length: 210.8 in; width: 78 in; wheelbase: 118 in

Price $3,163

Number produced 14,713

Edsel Pacer, 1958

Engine Standard: V-8 with overhead valves
361 ci
303 hp at 4,600 rpm
399 lb-ft at 2,800 rpm

Transmission Standard: manual gearbox with 3 speeds plus overdrive
Option: automatic 3 speed gearbox

Dimensions Length: 213 in; width: 79 in; wheelbase: 118 in

Price $3,028

Number produced 1,876

Edsel Corsair, 1959

Engine Standard: V-8 with overhead valves
332 ci
225 hp at 4,400 rpm
323 lb-ft at 2,200 rpm
Option: V-8 with overhead valves
361 ci
303 hp at 4,600 rpm
388 lb-ft at 2,900 rpm

Transmission Standard: 3 speed manual gearbox
Options: 3 speed automatic gearbox; 2 speed Mile-O-Matic automatic gearbox

Dimensions Length: 211 in; width: 79.8 in; wheelbase: 120 in

Price $3,072

Number produced 1,343

Cadillac Eldorado Biarritz, 1959

Engine	Standard: V-8 with overhead cylinder valves 390 ci 345 hp at 4,800 rpm 433 lb-ft at 3,400 rpm
Transmission	Standard: 4 speed automatic GM Dual Range Hydra-matic gearbox
Dimensions	Length: 225 in; width: 81 in; wheelbase: 130 in
Price	$7,401
Number produced	1,320

Edsel Ranger, 1960

Engine	Standard: V-8 with overhead valves 292 ci 185 hp at 4,200 rpm 291 lb-ft at 2,200 rpm Options: 6 cylinders in-line with overhead valves 223 ci 145 hp at 4,000 rpm 205 lb-ft at 2,000 rpm V-8 with overhead valves 352 ci 300 hp at 4,600 rpm 380 lb-ft at 2,800 rpm
Transmission	Standard: 3 speed manual gearbox Options: 2 speed automatic Mile-O-Matic gearbox; 2 speed automatic Fordomatic gearbox
Dimensions	Length: 216 in; width: 81.5 in; wheelbase 120 in
Price	$3,000
Number produced	76

Chrysler 300 F and 300 G, 1960/61

Engine	Standard: V-8 with overhead valves 413 ci 375 hp at 5,000 rpm 493 lb-ft at 2,800 rpm Option: 400 hp at 5,200 rpm
Transmission	Standard: 3 speed automatic Torque-Flite gearbox Option: 4 speed manual Pont-a-Mousson gearbox (300 F)
Dimensions	Length: 219.6 in; width: 79.4 in; wheelbase: 126 in
Price	$5,841 (300 F), $5,843 (300 G)
Number produced	248 (300 F), 337 (300 G)

Imperial Crown, 1961

Engine	Standard: V-8 with overhead valves 413 ci 350 hp at 4,600 rpm 469 lb-ft at 2,800 rpm
Transmission	Standard: 3 speed Torque-Flite automatic gearbox
Dimensions	Length: 227 in; width: 81.5 in; wheelbase: 129 in
Price	$5,774
Number produced	429

Cadillac Eldorado Biarritz, 1962

Engine	Standard: V-8 with overhead valves 390 ci 325 hp at 4,800 rpm 428 lb-ft at 3,100 rpm
Transmision	Standard: 4 speed automatic GM Hydra-matic gearbox
Dimensions	Length: 222 in; width: 80 in; wheelbase: 129.5 in
Price	$6,610
Number produced	1,450

Ford Thunderbird, 1962

Engine	Standard: V-8 with overhead valves 390 ci 300 hp at 4,600 rpm 425 lb-ft at 2,800 rpm Option: 340 hp at 5,000 rpm
Transmission	Standard: 3 speed automatic Cruise-O-Matic gearbox
Dimensions	Length: 205 in; width: 76 in; wheelbase: 113.2 in
Price	$4,788 (convertible), $5,439 (Sports Roadster)
Number produced	7,030 (convertible), 1,427 (Sports Roadster)

Chevrolet Corvair Monza Spyder, 1963

Engine	Standard: 6 cylinders flat, supercharged, mounted at rear 145 ci 150 hp at 4,400 rpm 209 lb-ft at 3,200 rpm
Transmission	Standard: 4 speed manual gearbox
Dimensions	Length: 180 in; width: 67 in; wheelbase: 108 in
Price	$2,798
Number produced	7,472

Studebaker Lark Daytona, 1964

Engine	Standard: V-8 with overhead valves 259 ci 182 hp at 4,500 rpm 259 lb-ft at 2,800 rpm Options: 198 hp at 4,500 rpm 289 ci with 213, 228, 240 and 290 hp 303 ci with 280 and 335 hp (with compressor)
Transmission	Standard: 3 speed manual gearbox

Studebaker Lark Daytona, 1964

Transmission

Options: Manual gearbox with 3 speeds plus overdrive; 4 speed manual gearbox; 3 speed automatic Flightomatic gearbox

Dimensions Length: 190 in; width: 71 in; wheelbase: 109 in
Price $2,805
Number produced Unknown

Chevrolet Corvette, 1965

Engine Standard: V-8 with overhead valves
327 ci
253 hp at 4,400 rpm
349 lb-ft at 2,800 rpm
Options: 304, 355, 370 or 380 hp; 396 ci, 430 hp at 6,400 rpm

Transmission Standard: 3 speed manual gearbox
Options: 4 speed manual gearbox; 2 speed automatic Power-glide gearbox

Dimensions Length: 175.2 in; width: 69.3 in; wheelbase: 98 in
Price $4,106
Number produced 15,376

Ford Mustang, 1965

Engine Standard: 6 cylinders in-line
200 ci
120 hp at 4,400 rpm
189 lb-ft at 2,400 rpm
Options: V-8 with overhead valves
289 ci
200 hp at 4,400 rpm, 281 lb-ft at 2,400 rpm
225 hp at 4,800 rpm, 304 lb-ft at 3,200 rpm
271 hp at 6,000 rpm, 312 lb-ft at 3,400 rpm

Transmission Standard: 3 speed manual gearbox
Options: 4 speed manual gearbox; 3 speed automatic Cruise-O-Matic gearbox

Dimensions Length: 181.6 in; width: 68.2 in; wheelbase: 108 in
Price $2,614
Number produced 101, 945 (1964–65)

Chevrolet Chevelle SS, 1966

Engine Standard: V-8 with overhead valves
396 ci
325 hp at 4,800 rpm
408 lb-ft at 3,200 rpm
Option: 360 hp at 5,200 rpm

Transmission Standard: 3 speed manual gearbox
Options: 4 speed manual Muncie gearbox; 2 speed automatic Powerglide gearbox

Dimensions Length; 197 in; width: 75 in; wheelbase: 115 in
Price $2,984
Number produced Unknown

Ford Fairlane 500, 1969

Engine Standard: 6 cylinders in-line
250 ci
157 hp at 4,000 rpm
240 lb-ft at 1,600 rpm
Option: V-8 with overhead valves
302 ci, 223 hp
351 ci, 253 and 294 hp
390 ci, 324 hp
428 ci, 340 hp

Transmission Standard: 3 speed manual gearbox
Options: 4 speed manual gearbox; automatic gearbox

Dimensions Length: 201 in; width: 74.4 in; wheelbase: 116 in
Price $2,851
Number produced 2,264

Cadillac Eldorado, 1976

Engine Standard: V-8 with overhead valves
500 ci
190 hp at 3,600 rpm
359 lb-ft at 2,000 rpm
Option: 215 hp with electronic injection

Transmission Standard: automatic GM Turbo Hydra-matic gearbox with 3 speeds

Dimensions Length: 224 in; width: 80 in; wheelbase: 126.3 in
Price $11,049
Number produced 14,000

Chevrolet Corvette, 1987

Engine Standard: V-8 with overhead valves
350 ci
240 hp at 4,000 rpm
344 lb-ft at 3,200 rpm

Transmission Standard: manual gearbox with 4 speeds plus overdrive on the last three
Option: 4 speed automatic gearbox

Dimensions Length: 176.5 in; width: 71 in; wheelbase: 96.2 in
Price $27,999
Number produced 10,625